Althar intense
Living the Paradox

Joachim Wolffram

Editor: Julia Horvath

Also available from Joachim Wolffram:
"Althar Intense – Space, Time, Veiling"
"Althar Intense – The Unconscious"

"For You – Records from Your Lives"
"The Free Human"

The Althar series:
Volume 1: "Althar – The Crystal Dragon"
Volume 2: "Althar – The New Magi"
Volume 3: "Althar – Towards Utopia"
Volume 4: "Althar – The Final Letting Go"
Volume 5: "Althar – Opus Magnum"

For information about audio recordings and workshops please visit:
www.wolffram.de
or
facebook.com/joachim.wolffram

Contents

Preface

The following text is a transcript of the messages Althar and Aouwa gave live during a ten-week online workshop in 2020 with 22 attendees from across the world. The meetings took place via Zoom on the last ten Sundays of the year.

Each of the weekly sessions lasted about ninety minutes and started with about thirty minutes of Cultivating the Awareness. Then Althar joined the group, gave a talk on a specific topic, and led an experiential journey to make his message as palpable as possible. The sessions were concluded with a typically brief Q&A. Parts of the Q&A that were on a more personal level as well as casual exchanges are not reproduced here.

Where necessary, the grammar or sentence structure has been corrected, and sometimes a few words have been changed or added to make a statement clearer.

Although the text is organized in paragraphs, there were many long pauses between the individual sentences. Also, oftentimes specific music was played to facilitate certain experiences. Since neither the speech rhythm nor the music can be captured adequately in a transcript, the audio recordings can be purchased at www.wolffram.de.

*

I would like to express my heartfelt gratitude to Julia Horvath for creating the initial transcript and the final editing.

Thank you, Julia!

*

You might consider reading this text at a very slow pace – ideally, one chapter per week.

*

1. The Living Trinity

We'll start with cultivating the awareness. We'll do this always, because cultivating the awareness is the single most important thing a human could do on the road to enlightenment, and even though I do not like repetition, I will repeat this within all these ten sessions. So we will always start with cultivating the awareness. The aim is to make you truly the master in your own physical house – the master of your emotions, thoughts, and feelings.

In order to start, it's good to take on an upright position, a position of royalty, and to be in an inner atmosphere of holiness. It's holy. It's something holy that you do. You're doing the highest that you can do as a human, you approach enlightenment, and you're determined to let go of whatever you believe is real. This is a really holy approach to existence.

It's important to use the body to facilitate this, for the body and the mind are so tightly interconnected. By bringing your body into a position of clarity, the mind follows. A position of clarity means you straighten the backbone, you straighten your neck, and you pull in your chin a little bit, which makes you feel like your crown is pushing into the sky. The shoulders are falling, just relax them, and just let them fall. The hands should be closed, meaning the fingers are not spread, but they touch each other. Place the left hand into the right hand and place them into your lap.

Okay, very important are also the eyes. The eyes are not fully closed and they are not fully open. They are three quarters closed, and they are gazing at approximately 45 degrees downwards. The reason for this is that then there is still some light coming through your eyes so you don't fall asleep; also, you are not so prone to dreaming. So, having your eyes a little bit open will make it much easier for you to stay aware. The mouth is closed. The tongue touches the roof of your mouth and your upper teeth. You are breathing through your nose, in and out.

I always emphasize that cultivating the awareness is a non-doing which is contrary to everything you do in your normal life. So, it's not about perfecting yourself, it's not about attaining anything, it's quite the contrary. It's coming back to your natural state, which is in fact, enlightenment. You come back to the natural state by stopping to act and react, and stopping to chase everything that comes up – by just being present.

Once you've taken on this position, start by becoming aware of your body. It's good to start with your feet. Your feet are touching the ground, they are carrying some weight, so just feel your feet. Become aware of your feet. And whenever you notice that something is getting between you and your feet, a thought, a noise from outside maybe, it doesn't matter, come back to the awareness of your feet.

Now include your lower legs in your awareness. These are parts of your body you usually never become aware of, they just exist. They carry you all the time, but now feel them. You may not have done this in years, unless you've had an accident or ache in your lower leg. Now become aware of them.

Feel your knees, and as you do, continue breathing through your nose.

Now include your upper legs in your awareness.

Now your buttocks. Feel the weight that they carry.

Feel your hands. It's very easy to put your awareness into your hands as opposed to your feet, isn't it? If you are a musician for instance, you have very fine control of your hands, for playing the piano or the guitar or the flute. The hands seem to be very close to you.

Now include both of your arms in your body awareness. It's like you are filling your body up with awareness, starting from your feet, and slowly, slowly, filling you up to your crown.

Feel your arms, and your shoulders. I always emphasize the shoulders because there are typically very tense. Right now, just be aware of your left shoulder, of the muscles going from your neck to your arm. Feel that region; feel deep into the tissue, and if you are sensitive you can feel how the tissue responds; it responds everywhere in the body, and as the body awareness gets closer to your head it becomes easier for you to sense. So, feel into the your shoulder, into the muscles, the skin.

As you place awareness anywhere in your body, the body responds. It recognizes you in a way, for the body contains you. It's a vessel for you. It's your temple in this reality. That's one of the many paradoxes we will talk about today. It's your temple.

How do you treat your body? Placing awareness in the body makes the body feel welcome by you. Typically, the human always fights with his body. He wants to dictate what it has to eat, how to digest, how to move. There is so much control, so much false thinking. The linear mind thinks it can control this super complex organism just because it knows a bit about chemistry. All of this is not necessary. The body is your friend, but you have to let it serve you. As you become aware of your body parts, you stop the fight, at least for a moment. Become content, and the body mirrors you. And vice versa, as the body relaxes, the mind will mirror the body. That's what awareness does. The body relaxes, and also the mind relaxes, reflecting the body.

Now feel into your right shoulder. When you do, you may sometimes feel warmth arising, but you just observe that. This is not about performing miracles or instant healing or anything like that. There is no expectation here. However, there are many, many fruits of being aware of your body, beyond your expectations, and they will come naturally. The less you interfere, the more easily they will come.

Good. Now feel your belly, your lower belly specifically. It may be moving a little. If your breath is deep, you feel a little bit of movement there; a slight movement.

Now move the awareness from your belly slowly upward to the solar plexus, oh what a center we have here. Just be aware of it. It's good to place your awareness also inside your body, not only on the outside, like on the skin, but also in the center. Feel everything, from the center outward. Feel your lungs. Feel the breath coming into the body, maybe it's a bit cold.

Now feel your throat, your tongue. There are many interconnections in the body, especially between the body and the mind, and the interconnection between the tongue and the mind is one of those that is important. The tongue is brought to calmness when it touches your upper teeth. It doesn't move any more.

Whenever you think, there are tiny movements in your tongue, always; same with the eyes. And vice versa, if you keep being aware of your tongue, it relaxes and the mind responds by relaxing as well. So feel your tongue. Relax your tongue.

Now feel your lips, all the muscles, all the tiny muscles surrounding your lips. Just relax them. How? Become aware of that region, place your awareness there.

Now the nose. Buddha became enlightened by observing his breath, and specifically by observing the area around his nose, because there is a high sensitivity, a very high sensitivity. In a way, it's easy to be totally aware of that region, as there is constant movement of the breathing air. Your awareness has a support through this.

Now feel your breath, be aware of your breath. Just let the breath come and go without trying to interfere. You do not want to breathe particularly deeply or lightly. Just let go of any control. And that's easier said than done.

As you get used to this, you will notice that the "in" breath will be comparatively short, and the "out" breath will be long. You will also notice that the breath becomes deeper, goes deeper into your belly, and that you breathe less frequently.

Everything becomes efficient if you just come to awareness, if you stop fighting yourself, stop fighting the outside world.

Now feel your eyes. I notice that mostly all of you have your eyes closed, and this is fine, because I am talking and distracting you anyway. But when you do this alone, try to keep your eyes a little bit open.

Now feel your crown, the top of your skull, your head.

When you sit upright, a vertical line is formed from the area between your genitals and the anus, the perineum, through the spine and through the skull. It's a straight line; an energy channel.

There's no need to go actively work with this, but there is a reason for this specific posture: the energy can flow. No need for you to do anything actively, everything flows on its own. Also, if you sit in an upright position you do not need any muscle energy to keep your body in balance. You simply don't need it. Thus, you can sit like this for a long time uninterrupted without the body crying out in pain or anything.

Now I want you to place your awareness into the center of your belly once again, three fingers below your navel in the center of your body, into the sacred region called the *Hara* or *Kikai Tan-den*.

One of the paradoxes is that there is no center anywhere in existence, but while the human is in this physical dream of having a body, there is a kind of body center which is here in the Hara. If you are rooted here, if you place your awareness here, you get very stable. Your emotions calm down, your mind is far away from this center; everything becomes silent, intuitive. Imagine in your hara a kind of light the size of a tennis ball and let the light expand. The light of your hara can expand beyond your body. It can give you tremendous stability.

In these sessions, I will always spend quite some time with the body awareness, but when you do this on your own, you can do it much faster. The main purpose of this is to become used to observing what goes on within you without reacting. That means that once you are in a stable position like you are now – you are grounded, you are in a way concentrated within your physical expression – then you let go of the concentration and switch to observation. Just becoming aware, not wanting anything, without any agenda.

You need a strong determination. As soon as you know you are taken away by whatever, let that go and come back to observation. This is the circuit breaker. The fundamental non-practice the human can do, to change his life, to go directly, directly, towards enlightenment. You stop acting out your patterns. That's true freedom.

The most fundamental thing in this non-practice is: do not judge yourself! You will realize a thousand times, when you do this practice for half an hour, that you have been distracted. But that isn't a problem! Just return to observation, or to the body awareness, grounding you once again. You will notice for instance that when you follow your thoughts, your inner movies, your body position will change. Your head will fall forward, the back bone will sink in; the body is in constant movement. So you come back to a position of clarity, you break the circuit of thinking. Come back to a position of clarity, and then you go back to observing.

We had long discussions, internally with some of my peers, about what to do in this ten week program. And I said, the most difficult thing for so many humans is to get beyond their mind.

There are a number of them who have never experienced being beyond their mind, and getting beyond the mind is way easier said than done.

So, if a human is stuck in his or her mind, they might acknowledge the wisdom they hear, but it remains on a conceptual level. Well, that is better than nothing. However, being able to get beyond the mind and to actually experience the wisdom that comes in, that is what makes this wisdom so potent. That is what illuminates the illusions.

Getting beyond the mind is not easy, but a prerequisite for it is what we are doing right now: being able to say in any instant to your thoughts, "Stop! No more! I do not cooperate. Right now, I am in pure awareness!" And even if Buddha comes along and wants to talk to you, you say, "Not now, my friend." If Althar comes along, chase him away. When you are cultivating the awareness, do not compromise with any interruption.

You might have seen the title that I placed on the entry slide. It said "Althar Intense Online," and then below that line it said "Living the Paradox." Living the Paradox is the headline for the next ten weeks, and we will partition the program roughly into two halves. In the first five sessions, we will focus on the human, on the human consciousness, on the human vessel; deconditioning it, or giving you the means to decondition yourself, and also to desensitize yourself, so that you are open for the high energies of higher consciousness.

Deconditioning also means loosening the core beliefs that you have to hang on to as a human, if you want to have shared experiences with others. So, you need certain core beliefs, for instance about time, space, gravity, and the firm belief of being a human being in the first place. If you did not have these core beliefs, you could not have human experiences. However, we will try to loosen these beliefs.

In the second half of this program, we will move to the "other side" so to speak and try to ground your consciousness in the realm beyond separation, enabling you to live on both sides simultaneously.

Good. That is the outline. I will be quiet for two minutes. We will then have some music, and Althar will join us. In these two minutes, be as aware as you can, and always come back to the awareness after each distraction.

*

I am Althar, the Crystal Dragon.

Back again, and it's so good to see you, even those of you who have not been with me in an in-person gathering, or the online gatherings we have done. We know each other. We know each other, and you know each other as a group, for as I say so often, humans orbit around each other, and sooner or later they meet again. They orbit through time, through the various realms; they travel in groups and some of them made a promise to realize embodied ascension. And here you are. You are amongst those who have the great desire to go into embodied ascension.

So, this is our first Althar Intense Online Program. And even though I carry the name Althar, I challenged Joachim to come up with another name, for he, just as you, will meld more and more the three levels that seem to exist from the perspective of separation: the absolute, the relative, and the in-between.

I, Althar, I am the "in-between." I am the bridge in consciousness, but this is changing. I have already melded with Joachim, and Aouwa is not that far away. It will become more and more natural for him to act as one and to no longer distinguish between the various levels. The same is true for you. You might feel often times like you are just a human, but you have other parts that are very present, and we will try to bring them in today. Also, you will change what you believe yourself to be and switch into a much, much grander role than you might think possible at the moment.

Joachim said in the beginning that getting beyond the mind might be the greatest hurdle; the greatest hurdle is opening up the mind and going beyond it. And one way to do this, one tool, is to use the imagination. Imagination! Now, I say right now that imagination is also of separation, so whatever you imagine within yourself, whatever you conjure up on your inner screen, is in a way still of separation. But we use illusions to illuminate illusions, you see. We can have imaginations that bring you into a different state of being, so that you can finally go beyond all imaginations, all false images, and eventually beyond separation.

We will have a lot of experiences in the coming weeks where we'll use the imagination, but I urge you right now not to stick to them, and to be ready to let them go. You might stick to the feeling, but not the circumstances that seem to have triggered the feelings, you see.

Today, we start with a metaphor that we use in the imagination. I will rely on this metaphor quite often – a sphere. If you look at the Zoom window and find Joachim's small video – you have to open your eyes to see it – you will see a sphere full of mirrors. I will use this symbol in what we are doing next.

Now you are fine to close your eyes again as Joachim does.

I want you to imagine a sphere, but without the mirrors. Let's say, a sphere of emptiness in emptiness, so it has no boundaries, although by means of your imagination you know that there is some boundary. This sphere in emptiness is very much like the entities who found themselves suddenly within separation. They did not know who they were, they didn't know anything. They were suddenly "there," but they had a desire, to be *something*. So, they had this shell around themselves that I call a sphere.

In their sphere, they also had consciousness and pure energy. Pure energy is a crystallized state of consciousness that reacts to the intents of consciousness.

Recall that consciousness has two main characteristics: it can be aware of itself, and it can have intents. And its intents are immediately mirrored by the pure energy.

Now, if an intent is repeated over and over and over again, you might say that it "solidifies," solidifies into what you call a belief. And a belief is nothing more than an intent that goes into auto repeat. It repeats itself constantly, constantly, constantly. Even if sooner or later the original intent may be forgotten, the resulting belief has nevertheless become stable. In our imagination and the metaphor I use, this is represented by a mirror on the surface of the sphere.

All the entities started out as empty spheres, but full of potential intents. And in a wish to know who they were, they started bringing forth intents and beliefs. They wanted a reflection of themselves; that is what pure energy does. And so they created the mirrors around themselves, and took them for real. That is the major insight: they took the reflection of pure energy for real.

If you could stop that today, you would be free. End of discussion!

But unfortunately, i's not that simple, because you, like all other entities, have already had a very, very long journey through separation, and in the process you have accumulated many, many, many beliefs.

These mirrors are, in a way, two way mirrors. They reflect to the outside, but also the consciousness within is reflected by them. Moreover, you might peer from inside through the mirrors, so that you see what is going on "out there."

Now imagine these spheres floating around, representing the entities with all their beliefs. They just want one thing: reflection. They want a reflection of themselves, and they want to be reflected by the others, for that stabilizes what they think they are. So they continue solidifying their mirror spheres and they call the reflections *me*. "This is me! This is what I am!" And they create mirrors in mirrors in mirrors.

When I say an entity goes into deeper density, you might equate it with adding more layers of mirrors. Thus, you don't just have one layer, like one shell around yourself, but you have multiple shells. It's getting denser and denser. It's like the Russian dolls; many, many layers, within layers, within layers.

Being a human means that you have incarnated on the lowest spectrum of consciousness, in the densest consciousness that can be experienced. So, it's not just a few layers that you just wash away and then suddenly you see things as they are, it doesn't work that way. There are a multitude of layers. So, letting go is not a onetime thing. Therefore, the deconditioning is so important. With deconditioning, you start dissolving the mirrors by not validating them anymore.

Now, look at this construct of a mirror sphere. It's interesting. It's a paradox in many respects. The paradox is that you understand this on a conceptual level, and you want to get out, you want to get beyond this mirror prison. At the same time, you wish for embodied ascension, meaning you want to be *beyond* it, but still be *in* it somehow.

You want to be in the dream, and out of the dream. You want to be in the water, and out of the water. This is in a way a paradoxical situation, because it doesn't really work. Yet, in a way we can make it work, in a "semi dreaming" state.

On the other hand, this metaphor shows that it's not easy to get out, for if you have the intent to get out, the true intent, and therefore you want to do something to get out, what actually happens?

Usually, you end up creating just another mirror, or even another layer of mirrors. Then you might call yourself spiritual, or religious, or whatever. But you're doing it out of a lack. You feel a lack, you want to compensate for the lack, so you *do* something, and you create another mirror or another layer of mirrors and this can go on for lifetimes. Oh, you may dissolve a few layers, but at the same time you create new ones. You see yourself as a Christian, as a Jew, as whatever, and so you go on and on.

You also cannot fight these mirrors, for what happens if you break a mirror? Well, you have a lot of shards continuing mirroring yourself. It's a difficult situation.

But there's another paradox upon which we rely heavily: *you can shift out of separation in an instant!* This is something that is really hard to understand, but you can experience it. It seems illogical, but it works! You can shift out of your human condition instantly and see it from the outside; see things as they truly are, beyond time. Sooner or later you will be drawn back into your human mirror cabinet, but if you have experienced at least once such a timeless moment beyond separation, it will have a tremendous impact on your consciousness, on your understanding, on your determination. This is what I call a "moment of enlightenment."

A moment of enlightenment takes place beyond time. Then you might ask, "Well, is it possible to be in a constant state of enlightenment?"

And I say, "Yes, yes, in principle. But it is difficult." In principle, you could compose like Mozart. You take a sheet of paper, you take a pencil and draw these little tiny black dots and you have a symphony like Mozart does, and Mozart says, "What's the point? I'm doing it all the time."

But there are certain preconditions for constant enlightenment to happen. While you are in time, you keep hanging on to certain beliefs. So I urge you, I challenge you, to let go of every expectation of how your journey will unfold in time; for actually, it doesn't really matter.

At every moment, you have the option to switch out, to have a moment of enlightenment, beyond time.

So, do not ask, "When will my permanent enlightenment take place?" Don't even think along these lines, for you would just say, "Well, I'm here, on a timeline; I'm waiting for something, because I am not content with what is." But this is just another mirror. Forget about that! Accept things as they are. Go to the awareness. Go to the deconditioning and be prepared to experience moments of enlightenment beyond time. And then wait and see what comes in time.

I know this is difficult, for the human wants so much to just flip a switch and be in a constant state of enlightenment, but it just doesn't work that way – and it should be a great relief for you to hear that! So, abandon that expectation and go for the moments of enlightenment. Everything else comes by itself.

It's not a question of how old you are, or what you did before, or how many languages you speak, nothing like that. Everybody can do it! Everybody can do it, and we will do it here over and over again.

In a way, some might say, "But Althar, all of this just takes place in my imagination. It is not real". And I say, yes, maybe. *So what?*

Everything in separation is false. But you have a certain feeling when you move toward liberation, toward less illusions. You feel the opening up. And when you are ready to let go of *everything*, no matter what you perceive even in your moments of enlightenment, if you are fundamentally ready to let go of everything, then you accept that everything in separation is made up. Use this understanding as a tool to go beyond the mind and you'll have liberating experiences that transform your daily life as a human. And from there, you proceed in your letting go, until you arrive at the final letting go.

It's so simple. There is no expectation involved, there is no dogma. There is no priest, no guru, no religion, no nothing. It is just you. *It is just you!* And it is you who has to do it; nobody can do it for you. Not I, Althar, not anybody else. You have to let go. And that is why we insist so much on cultivating the awareness, for this is the fundamental tool. I cannot do it for you, but I can challenge you to do it, I can challenge you to let go of all your notions, and I will challenge you in these coming weeks. Every session, I will challenge you. That is what I can do.

Actually, I do not really care how you will react. Ideally, you see the opportunity. Ideally, you withstand the eye of the dragon, you face it. Ideally, you are ready to go into the fire and see what remains when everything burns down. I guarantee you: what remains is the purest you that you have ever witnessed, that you have ever experienced.

So I will challenge you over and over again in these ten weeks. It's your time, and your opportunity to go as deep, maybe even deeper, than ever before. It's your opportunity to ground the wisdom that you might hold on the conceptual level and bring it into an experienced reality. And only then does it become true wisdom.

Now, in a way we are already in a specific dimension beyond your human sphere, your human earthly sphere, in a dimension of our own. And from this perspective, I ask you to picture the mirror sphere that you call your human existence in this lifetime. Take a moment. Picture this sphere.

There is no right or wrong in this. You might see the mirrors. You might even see movies playing in the mirrors. It's up to you. Take a second and feel it. See all the facets of you that mirror you.

Good. As we continue, I will play some music, for the music is so good for the imagination. It enhances the imagination.

(*Music plays*)

See your "human existence" sphere, the "you."

Now, dive into that sphere. Do not dive into your human body, but into the sphere that you call yourself. Now you are right next to where your human body is sitting right now. Oh no, you don't see the mirrors as we've seen them on the sphere Joachim has shown in the camera. But still, you see reflections of yourself – you have decorated your room to your liking, you might have photos standing here or there, or hanging on the wall. Everything reflects you.

Have a look at your physical body. The physical body is the greatest mirror cabinet of all. It's constantly, constantly mirroring itself. Your eyes see the arms, and the legs, and you conclude, "Oh, this is my body". You feed it, you feel it. You think that you think with it. It's a mirror cabinet; mirrors everywhere.

All these mirrors play their role essentially through your perceptual process. Whatever you perceive had to pass these mirrors and was reflected back and forth between them. So in a way, you are like a shard in a kaleidoscope; you see yourself everywhere, constantly.

What is real in all of this? All the false identities that you have created in this lifetime, they are not real, but you needed them for survival. You needed them for social interaction. You needed them to follow your ambitions. See, this is not a judgement. It's just seeing how things truly are. As you hover in your personal sphere and watch it, you can see all of that, you can see all the mirrors. And you can make the choice that you want to become free of them. It doesn't mean you shred them or crush them. No, you shouldn't do that – you want to continue your life. But you do not want to be the slave of them anymore. You can stop validating them over and over again. You can stop craving to be validated. Let those false identities dissolve. Continue to act, but as a free human.

In this moment, you are right next to your human body, in your human sphere, full of mirrors and reflections, beliefs, and core beliefs. Now expand outwardly. Just like this. See the sphere from the outside, as we have done before – instantly – do not ask how, just do it, imagine it. See, this is what I meant earlier, you can get out of it in an instant. And once you are outside of your personal sphere, you are way freer than before.

Now, expand. Expand! What does it mean to expand? Well, you are formless, so expand your formlessness.

As you do, you might see more spheres, similar to your human sphere, for of course every human has his or her own sphere. Just see them. They are like a vast field, a vast field of spheres. It's not just you; there are so many humans.

You see, I say consciousness is holographic. All the humans in their respective spheres see the same movies on their mirrors, and they conclude that they are all together in the same realm sharing experiences, but are they really? Are they really?

They are sitting in their sphere, dreaming of nicer mirrors, larger mirrors, more comfortable mirrors, and dreaming of achieving something in time. They are even dreaming of becoming free, dreaming of enlightenment. And whatever they do, they just produce more mirrors and more mirrors, until they are ready to embrace the simplicity; ready to embrace the simplicity of understanding the fundamental principles of consciousness – intent and reflection – but not making the reflection real. Seeing it as what it is – a reflection that is not real, but made up.

As you see all these other humans in their individual spheres, you recognize that there is not so much difference between you and the others. They are dreaming of life as a human. It's like being in a cocoon. You might even say that the whole Second Round of Creation takes place in any of those spheres.

Now, in a manner of speaking, increase your vibration; perceive on finer levels. Expand more and more. As you do, you might see or imagine other spheres, spheres of non-physical entities. And guess what, guess what? They are also in their mirror-spheres. Maybe their spheres are not that dense, but they are also inside their own spheres.

However, it is the human who can go beyond his sphere, for if you understood the principle of separation in the densest density possible, then, *you know that you know!* You know that there is no escape *within* separation. In a way, you could say that you have experienced *all* of separation! You have looked everywhere and came to the conclusion that within separation there isn't any freedom, or any peace. *Separation isn't real.*

Those non-physical entities, well, they still have to shed their illusions. Some of them are here to assist and they know that they will incarnate sooner or later. Some of them have already been incarnated and they are here waiting for their next steps. But never ever be influenced too much by those on the other side who claim to explain to you how things work; that you should follow them through the next step of evolution, follow in their footsteps. Ask yourself: do they lead you *beyond* separation, or just into a different experience *within* separation?

You have been here in the non-physical for eons and that is why you incarnated. You did not incarnate to eventually come back into the non-physical, but in a manner of speaking, to come out on "the other side."

Now, expand even more. Expand even more.

Let go of all appearances. Just *be*. You are beyond space, you are beyond time. And paradoxically, beyond time your true self has already ascended.

Do not try to understand this mentally! Do not try to dissect this! You are still here as a human, in time, in your human experience, and think you have to do something or you have to get enlightened, so that your true self can ascend. But from beyond time, this has already happened, you see.

So, connect with your true self. Be in communion. Feel the simplicity; the simplicity of just being, being in suchness; nothing to prove, nothing to protect. Also, be in communion with your human facet sitting in the chair or couch right now. It's similar to the beginning of the session, when you felt your various body parts at the same time, like your feet and your crown. Well, it's not that different now. Feel your true self and feel your human self, your human aspect, and feel everything in between.

This is what I call the bridge in consciousness. I, Althar, call myself a bridge in consciousness. Right now, you are exactly that. The bridge in consciousness is a knowingness that never leaves you. It's the knowingness that separation is not real and that there is not only a way out, but in a way, you are already out! It's the knowingness of clarity, of compassion with yourself and all of existence. It's a knowingness of the utmost strength, for you know that nothing can withstand pure consciousness.

The false cannot be maintained in the light of truth. It's impossible.

And these are exactly the characteristics that the human oftentimes associates with a dragon: clarity, strength, being unrelenting, being compassionate.

Before Joachim made contact with me, he had an experience like this. He saw me, or his mind converted me into pictures. He saw me sitting somewhere, say, in outer space or on some mountain top, waiting. Waiting and waiting, for eons – so it seemed to him. Until at some point I just spread my wings and descended. And he was very impressed by that for the waiting was without effort.

At that point he did not really realize that I was beyond time, so what appeared to his human eye to be an eon, was nothing for me, it's a shift in perspective. But when the time was right, I descended. And now it's time for you. You are a bridge in consciousness. It has no form, but you can give it a form. It doesn't really matter what form you choose, but for these ten weeks, choosing a dragon makes our language much easier. So, from now on, whenever I speak of your dragon, I refer to what you are right now – a bridge in consciousness.

Your formlessness expands into the absolute and the relative. Now give form to your formlessness, as a dragon, no matter how you picture it. It's fluid; it can change, it's certainly not fixed.

And now, descend back into density, back into density without fear, for you know who you are.

See all these entities, these non-physical entities, oh they are in awe. Few of them understand what is going on, but most can feel there is something special happening.

Now, find your human mirror-sphere. Dive directly into it, and see your human sitting there. Envelop it, be all around your human, and permeate it; be in and around it. The clarity, the compassion, the knowingness – all is here. It doesn't need any reflection, it doesn't need any perception, it's not bound to mirrors; it's your natural state.

Oh yes, this dragon might shine a light on many portions of you that you do not like too much, but so what? Let all of them come forth, peacefully. You see, it is *you* who makes all of them real. Every emotion that you have comes from you. There is nobody else dictating what emotions you should have. It is *you!* You can let these aspects and incidences go; you can hand them over to your dragon. And the dragon just looks at them and overlooks them for they are not real.

The dragon doesn't care for illusions, and it doesn't care for *your* illusions. Hand them over, and they dissolve into pure energy.

Now as we are sitting here, in this wonderful and multi-functional symbol of a sphere, also imagine your true self as a shining sphere, like a sun.

A sun that is beyond space, so dimensions and extensions don't make any difference. See it as a shining ball of light, and let it come close.

You see, true self has no fear. It is not that true self enters separation, but in your imagination you bring it here. Let it come closer, and closer and closer; the size of an orange maybe. Let it enter through your crown. Be aware of your crown, you know how to do that, and feel true self entering through it; slowly, slowly. As it enters through your body, its light shines. It is the light of pure consciousness, of pure beingness. And again, the body responds and relaxes. Let this ball of light sink into your chest, your heart. Feel it there, feel your awareness of your body; feel the relaxation.

Now let it sink into your belly.

Now let it grow. Let your true self, this ball of light – this pure consciousness that you are – grow. In a way, it is a sphere without a boundary. It envelops you and the dragon. Allow them to meld. Let go of the distinction between human, dragon, and true self.

This is a moment of living the trinity.

This is a moment of living the paradox.

Now let go of all the images that I gave you. Just be with the feeling – only the feeling – the living trinity becoming the one you.

What did we just do? We just used the simplicity of consciousness in our favor, starting with the body, calming it. Then, we held a few intents that were mirrored so you could feel them. Then we applied knowingness to all your beliefs and saw them for what they really are. And suddenly, there is a moment where they are just gone; a moment of enlightenment, a moment of living the paradox.

*

I said I will challenge you throughout these ten weeks, and the first challenge you will experience is *not* trying to repeat in your memories the experience you just went through. You can repeat it, but then do it for real. Do not replay a movie of it! Let it be fresh, always, always fresh.

There will be times when you feel like you want to repeat it and you don't arrive at it. But I challenge you not to try to force it. Instead, just come back to cultivating your awareness, let your intents go, let your ambitions go.

Do not create a memory, a new mirror, from your current experience.

In a way you might say that the coming ten weeks are already contained in distilled form in this first session. However, we will go into much more depths and attempt to ground the wisdom in your experienced reality.

I know you want to stay in this wonderful feeling, but I challenge you to listen to me. Instead of naming something as "homework," I call it a *challenge*. I challenge you to cultivate your awareness everyday in the next ten weeks. Ideally, do this right after getting up. Take thirty minutes just for yourself. Don't find any excuses, just do it! The trick with doing it in the morning is that you cannot complain you have no time. Just get up earlier! It's so easy, and I promise you that for every minute you cultivate your awareness you need two minutes less sleep. So it's a good deal anyway. And it's the basis, *the* basis for becoming a free human, a free spirit, and to realize embodied ascension.

There is a second challenge, a second homework I want you to consider. Multiple times a day, whenever it occurs to you, just stop internally and check your feeling reality. What are you doing in the moment, what are you feeling? What is your body language, where are tensions in your body? Just become aware of it, for two, three, five seconds, and then continue with what you have been doing. Just get in the habit of being aware of what you do throughout the day.

My ambition is truly, truly to inspire you to go beyond, over and over again. I, Althar, I have no interest in doing a lovely session once a week just to have a good time, to feel good and sugar coat things. You can find that anywhere. So, please, dedicate this time to yourself. Also, the end of the year, like we have right now, is a miraculous time – it's a time of rebirth.

It's a great honor for me to be with you on this journey. It's a longtime dream that Joachim has

had, and I have had, and that Althar the Atlantean
has had. It's the dream of waking up from the
dream of separation.

I am Althar. I will be with you next Sunday,
thank you.

2. False Identities and the Emotional Body

Let's start with cultivating the awareness. Meanwhile, you've gotten used to it, I assume. Start by taking on a royal posture; a posture of clarity. That means you stretch the backbone, stretch your neck, push your head up a little bit, and you pull in your chin. Your backbone forms a straight line. Because you're sitting up straight, you don't need muscle strength to stabilize your posture. So your whole upper body can relax. You can hand it over to gravity. So you sit naturally in a royal posture, without any effort.

The fingers are closed; you might place your hands inside each other, or place them on your legs, as you like. It's very important to have the eyes three quarters closed. If you leave them a little bit open so that some light comes in, then you don't fall asleep so easily and don't go into dreamland right away.

Good. The mouth is closed. The breath comes in and out through the nose. Start with observing the breath as it enters your nose. It comes into your body, into your lungs.

As always, I emphasize that cultivating of the awareness is a non-doing. This means we do not try to achieve anything or to perfect anything – not your breath, not your posture, nothing. All this comes naturally. It's coming back to the natural state by stopping doing. And in order to be able to stop doing, it's good to have some points on which you can focus on to come into an inner mindset of clarity and stability. Then, we also let go of that, we'll just let go of everything.

Now feel both of your feet and your lower legs simultaneously. Just place your awareness in that area. You might feel light sensations; the texture of your socks for instance. It might feel warm or cold down there. Just observe. Just observe what's going on in that area.

Now include your knees and your upper legs. Again, be aware of the sensations going on there. Include your buttocks, your genitals, and your anus. Even if it sounds strange, try to relax your anus, and see what happens with the interior of your body when you do.

Include your fingers in your awareness. You might start with the fingertips, all ten of your fingertips. Not the full hand, just the fingertips.

Awareness is a beautiful thing. It can be everywhere at the same time. It can be in a single place. It can focus on certain parts, or it can include other parts. It's very flexible.

Slowly, slowly expand from your fingertips, and include your entire hand in your awareness. Again, become aware of the sensations that you feel here.

A sensation is like a raw impulse. It could be an itching, heat, a pulsing, a touch, a light pain. Sensations are not yet distorted by associations, they are still raw. They are not yet processed by other parts of your consciousness. If you are in full awareness, you can become very aware of them, and you might notice how a sensation turns into something else; into an emotion, a feeling.

Now include both of your arms in your awareness.

Now place your awareness in your belly; the place of safety, of stability. Feel how your lower belly is massaged while you are breathing. The diaphragm moves and massages lightly the whole belly area.

As you settle in your belly, the area of your Hara, your mind calms down. Everything becomes quieter and slower. Stress fades, hecticness fades.

Now include your chest in your awareness. It's constantly moving as you breathe.

Now be very aware of the skin on your back. This is a very sensitive area; it has to be. You can't see there, so you must have feelers that check what's going on behind your back. Your skin is very sensitive.

Now sense your throat. There are so many blockages in the throat. As you put your awareness there, everything relaxes, tensions vanish; expression becomes natural, unhindered.

Now include your shoulders, your lips, and the inside of your nose. Feel how the air flows in and out.

Include your eyes. Sense what's going on in the muscles surrounding your eyes.

Now sense the skin of your forehead, specifically between your eyebrows. As you become aware of that region, it relaxes, and it has an immediate impact on your mind, on your inner sight.

Now sense your crown.

Good. Now become aware of the totality of your body; from the crown to your feet; the surface and the interior. Once you are aware of the totality of you, go into observation mode. Just observe, forget about the various body parts, and regions, and muscles, and skin. Just observe what is going on, what appears on your inner screen.

The moment you become aware of something, you recognize it as what it is, and you let it go.

Letting go is something inactive. You do not push it away or try to suppress it. Not at all. You become aware of a phenomenon, but you do not follow it. You do not react to it, nor do you add any energy to it. You step out of it. You are the observer, untouched.

You can observe how a stimulus coming from some sensation of your body, a raw impulse, is suddenly turned into a series of associations. It triggers, say, an inner movie, and you are tempted to be drawn into it. However, as soon as you realize that you are drawn in, you just step out, without judgment.

Now I want you to become aware of your breath again. When the inhalation turns into the exhalation, there is a subtle impulse that takes place and vice versa. So let the breath come and go, and feel as precisely as you can all the muscles that change with the impulse of the change in breath. Be very vigilant. Try not to miss the turning points.

When you focus on this instant, when you try to capture it, you can see all the thoughts that are coming forth, telling you what you have to do in order to observe the next turning point. You feel some tension arising within you, although the attempt to observe is still passive. It requires no activity. You do not need to control your breath. Yet, all these thoughts are instantly arising and create a tension. So even if you don want to do anything actively, there is still some kind of disturbance of the natural rhythm. But should you try to actively control or "perfect" your breath, then everything only becomes much more complicated.

It is a very good exercise to try to be aware of these turning points in your breath, because then you feel all these subtle mechanisms. Also, then you notice very easily when you start to dream. "Oh, I missed the moment again, interesting, where have I been?"

Cultivating the awareness is the number one practice. It's the deconditioning. It's the liberation in the moment. The sooner you are able to break the chain reaction that starts with a stimulus and all that comes after it – associations, emotions, and all the rest of that – the easier the letting go becomes.

If, for whatever reason, you are in a state of rage already, then it's difficult to calm down, because there are already all the chemicals floating through your body. For instance, where Joachim is right now, there are a lot of noises. Somewhere there is a family fight going on. It's not that easy for him to concentrate. At the same time, it's much easier to let go if you are aware of the noises and do not automatically go into complaining mode. So it's about coming back to the awareness, over and over again.

Today's topic is false identities and the emotional body. We will bring in Althar and he will say a few words about this.

*

I am Althar, the Crystal Dragon.

It is a great pleasure to gather with you for this second meeting of our ten-week intense program.

We've said in the beginning that in the first half of these ten weeks, we will have a deeper look at the human vessel and that we want to loosen all the beliefs that you hold concerning this vessel.

This means that we try to bring into experience what you already know. So in this session, I am going to repeat things that you most likely have heard about. You may have read about them in the Althar books or elsewhere. Still, it is about bringing this knowledge into experience and seeing what it means to go beyond these beliefs.

Today we will talk about identification. The human identifies on many levels, the two most important of which are the human body and what I call the emotional body.

So, let's start with the human body. I've said frequently that the human body is the densest form of existence an entity can experience. In order to go beyond separation, we all deemed it necessary that an entity incarnates in flesh, because then, only at the densest densities of all, can he verify for himself that there is no true creation to be found in separation. Otherwise, there would have been a doubt, like, "Maybe, if I went to that density, I might have found the Holy Grail" – or whatever the masterhood of everything is. So, the entities had to come to Earth in order to truly have a chance to get enlightened beyond any doubt.

Now, incarnating is really difficult, because consciousness and matter have to merge somehow, and we had to help a little bit so that you finally came to the belief that you are a body. For a human like you, it feels natural to be identified partly with your human body, with your human expression. But have a deeper look at this body, for now it is time to loosen this identification.

Have a look at that body. What is it precisely? You will see immediately that you cannot really fathom it.

You were working with your breath a few minutes ago, the breath that enters your lungs. Some of the molecules of the air that you have just breathed in will become part of your physical body. Other molecules will leave your physical body as you breathe out. So, is the breath within your lungs part of your body?

Oh, it's close to becoming part of your body, so very close, but is it yet? Further, if you had no air to breathe, your body would die immediately. So, what would you say, is the air that you need to survive, to sustain yourself, part of you?

It's the same with the cells. There are so many cells in your body. Seventy billion of your cells are exchanged every day, that is, they die and are recreated. Feel that for a moment. *Seventy billion per day.* This makes roughly *eight hundred thousand per second.* Consider that! There is a constant dying and rebirthing within your body.

I'm pretty sure you've never noticed it; not a single death of a cell have you ever witnessed. The body is in constant change, a constant state of flux. It is absolutely transient, impermanent, yet there is the natural impulse to say, "This is me!" And "this is me" means implicitly that there is something that is "not me."

What do you actually know of your body? What do you really know of your body? If you want to move a hand, what do you do? Do you dive into your brain and trigger some neurons, add some chemicals here and there? No, certainly not. You just have the intent, and then the miracle of consciousness sets in. It reflects the intent to move your hand in physical reality, and your hand moves. You do not know how you do that! Yet, you still call it your body.

The same holds for your digestion. Oh, you might have heard how the stomach adds certain chemicals to the food that you have swallowed, but do you really have a clue how that works? How the nutrients are extracted and absorbed? Do you do any of that actively? You don't. The body does it for you somehow.

The digestion is also very interesting, for the whole digestive tract is a kind of "hollowness" within you. You put something into your mouth; your mouth is hollow. Then the food more or less falls into your stomach and falls out again at the buttocks. There is hollowness within you. Is that hollowness a part of your body, or would you say, "No it's not. This is *not* me even though it is *within* me."

Or you might say, the body is the totality of all the cells that carry your DNA. But then you have to realize that there are as many cells in your body that do *not* carry your DNA, and that are definitely *not* you in that respect. Yet, without these other cells living in your body, you wouldn't survive a single moment.

So, what *is* the body, in essence? It's very hard to say. The body is a convenience construct. It's practical to have the notion of a body in your physical reality, for instance if you want to reserve a seat. You simply need some space for your physical vehicle to sit somewhere. But still, it is really difficult to say what the body is, for it is in a constant change of flux; nothing of your body is constant.

There is another highly interesting identification that you carry with you. It is with what I call the emotional body. Joachim talked a bit about sensations that you can become aware of. Sensations are all the impulses coming through your physical sense organs. Then, on the other end of the spectrum, you have feelings.

In my terminology, feelings are impersonal. Feelings like beauty, peace, or love – they are impersonal. They are, in a way, also raw. They are undistorted.

And then there are emotions. Emotions are personal. Emotions are always in relation to what you think you are. It might be an emotion of satisfaction, or annoyance, anger, pride, sympathy, shame... These are emotions. And where do the emotions come from? They are created by what you think you are. They are made by the false identities that you believe yourself to be.

In the last session, we spoke about the desire of entities to establish stable reflections of themselves. When you are incarnated as a human, these stable reflections are what I call the false identities. This is the façade that you carry with you. The façade that you believe to be, or that you want others to believe that you are. This is what you show to others, and because this façade is not real, well, it has to be reestablished over and over again.

Now, if somebody comes along and validates your façade by saying, "I like what you are doing, and you are looking good today", well, then you are pleased. You get emotional satisfaction and you tend to like that person. On the contrary, if somebody rejects you, rejects your façade, then you get easily angry, and you tend to dislike that person.

This is where the emotions come from. They drive you. This is the way I use the term emotion. They are personal, as opposed to feelings, and sensations.

When I say "Feel into you," you typically do not check to see if you still have two arms and two

47

legs, which are components of your physical appearance. No, you go within and you check out your emotional state. How are you feeling in this very moment? What are your emotions? Are you satisfied, are you angry? Are you calm, are you at peace? That is what you identify the most with, and that is what you care about the most. This is the emotional body.

Your emotional body is the totality of all your false identities! In a really paradoxical way, you cannot see your emotional body even though it's much more relevant to your daily experiences than your physical body.

There are many traditions that deal with the various subtle bodies, like the emotional body, the mental body, and all the rest of that. I tend to not go into that, because then it can easily become an ambition to optimize your various bodies, bring them all into harmony and all the rest of that. And I do not say that this is wrong – it can be very, very helpful. However, at a certain point it's best to just let go of all these discernments. The magic of pure awareness brings everything into harmony anyway, without you needing to take care of the details!

Well, knowing about the details may not harm, but it's much easier to let them go and to let nature do its natural thing. You will be coming back into harmony without knowing the details. Just as you don't know how your arm is moving, you just don't need to know about all the subtle bodies and how they are suddenly harmonizing with them-selves, other than becoming aware of it.

With the emotional body, however, I make an exception, because it's a very, very crucial ele-ment in the human experience. This is what you fight for. This is what you yourself believe to be. This is what defines you as a human being!

In one of my earlier messages I said, "The mo-ment you dissolve your emotional body, you stop being a limited human." You stop being a limited human, and quite frankly, you can hardly even be called a human anymore, for you have liberated yourself. Without an emotional body, without re-acting to any stimulus that comes from the outside and relating it to the history of yourself, the his-tory of your false identities, without all of that, you are free to act as you like.

This is, of course, much, much easier said than done.

You tend to despise the false identities that you carry with you. Some of them you might know. Maybe it is a leftover from your teenage days, it may come from a fear you might have covered up, or from an experience you had as a young child. You know about these false identities, but you try to suppress them, to push them away, not to let them come to the forefront. And then there are false identities that you *do* like. You *want* to be like them. The spiritual person, the wise person – whatever it is that you want to be – and you pam-per these false identities.

That's just the way it is, and it's very, very difficult to get beyond that.

*

Let's see the emotional body in action right now. I know all of you have read about the emotional body, practiced with it, learned about it. Now, what if I say: at the end of this segment, three of you will be chosen to have three minutes uninterrupted to express their highest wisdom. It will be transcribed, published, and can be read for all eternity.

What happens within you right now? Nobody knows if he or she is going to be picked, but three will be picked.

Observe what's going on within you.

This is when all the false identities come to the forefront. You might have had a bad experience long ago, when, say, as a child you were picked and had to come to the front of the class. Maybe you had to sing, and it didn't work that well. So you decided, "I don't like doing things in public, like singing, or even speaking," and then, as a consequence of that bad experience, you always tried to avoid coming into such a situation in the first place. You might not even be aware of that. It's an aspect that is triggered within you whenever there is a slight chance you might be asked to speak in public. So, you didn't go where that could have happened. You found a "rational" reason for not going there, without even knowing the underlying real reason for your choice.

These false identities, these aspects, are influencing you to this very day without you knowing it.

Another aspect within you might say, "Well, I like to express. It's time that I express my wisdom for anybody to hear."

But a third aspect comes in and says, "I would love to do that, but my English is not so good. I would be stuttering and that's not what I want to do in front of others."

In fact, the emotional body is highly complex. It's not just one false identity in the foreground. Typically, there are a huge number of false identities active at any time, and they are in conflict with each other. One wants this, the other wants that. Depending on your own awareness, depending on your own stability, it is really difficult to remain clear in this turmoil. You can fluctuate between fear and desire, back and forth, all the time.

All of you know that, and most likely you don't like that. Still, the question remains: How do we get beyond? How do we get beyond the false identities? And this is something that shouldn't be taken lightly, for what we are attempting here is like deconstructing a house of cards without it collapsing.

Every identification is false! That is why I emphasize the notion false identity. Because everything, everything, everything in separation is transient and impermanent, it doesn't make any sense to say, "I identify with something," because that something is changing constantly.

Still, as you are living in this physical human dream, you need a vessel to interact through; you need a vessel to survive. You want to experience enlightenment, and you want to experience "going beyond" without dying!

So, you need to be very careful when dissolving the false identities. You cannot just crush the emotional body, and quite obviously it doesn't suffice to just know about its mechanics. But, knowing about the mechanics, knowing how a stimulus that comes in is converted by a false identity into an emotion that validates or rejects you and what you think you are – if you know about all of this then you can slowly, slowly free yourself.

That is why I emphasize so much cultivating your awareness, for that is the cornerstone of liberation.

*

Let's have a small experience now. Not as long as last time, but let's have a small experience. And we'll play some music for it.

(Music plays)

In the last session, I used the metaphor of the sphere covered with mirrors, and I spoke of the Russian doll principle to illustrate that the human has much more than just a single surface layer. Instead, the human has many, many surface layers. One such layer is what you might call your emotional body.

Now, imagine yourself within a sphere as we

have used in the last session, but now we replace the surface, which were mirrors, with stained glasses, as you have, say, in churches. Each window depicts a certain scene. In a church, this is typically something around Jesus being born or being crucified. You have wonderful scenes and horrible scenes.

Now, in your sphere, you have also many of these stained glass windows. They all depict you at various stages of your life. There are so many scenes! You might say that every experience you have ever had has left a small imprint in your emotional body by means of such stained glass windows. Sometimes, a huge number of these stained glass windows are combined to form a false identity or a persona, but there are many, many, many windows that are more or less isolated. They represent incidences that happened at some point in your life. Also, there are some stained glass windows that came with you from your past lifetimes. These result from experiences that were so traumatic that you couldn't even let them go when you died your last physical death. So, you brought them with you, not even knowing about them.

Now, picture yourself inside this sphere, surrounded by all these stained glass windows. In the center of this sphere is a spotlight that emits a bright light. When the light falls on one of those stained glass windows, the story captured in the window comes to life. It's reenacted. It's an aspect of you, a false identity, a scene in your life, and you feel again what happened back then. It's a time bubble; it's a story frozen in time. Yet, when you shine some light on it, it is replayed; it replays and you feel what went on back then.

Whenever a stimulus hits your sphere, the spotlight moves and illuminates a window that you associate with the stimulus.

Maybe you liked the birth of your child, but the death of your parent was not that nice. Maybe you had an accident resulting in a lot of pain, or maybe you won the lottery at some point in time. These stories may come to life at any time.

And there is your professional false identity. It's huge, there are many pieces of stained glass in it, a lot of small windows. That's what you take on when you go to work and talk to clients, or customers, or your colleagues. You bring these windows to life, and you also pierce through them, through the windows, and see what the others see of you. You want to show them a specific façade so you highlight it, and you are very receptive to what others think of you. Do they validate you? Do they see you the way you want to be seen? If yes, you are in an emotion of happiness, maybe calmness. If they reject you, if a client yells at you, it might be different, for you want this façade of yours to be acknowledged.

But because you ultimately just want *something* about you to be real, acceptance and rejection are basically equivalent. For what would you be if no one took note of your false identities, your wonderful stained glass windows, and reacted to them *somehow*? A being of the second round of creation wants reflections of itself, it wants a vessel of mirrors to live in and to experience through.

The number one step towards enlightenment is not only seeing this for what it is, but making the choice not to be a slave anymore to any stimulus coming from the apparent outside!

Oh yes, you need a certain kind of façade to play the human game, *but you stop making it real!* You stop believing that *this is you,* just as you stop believing that you are your body, for you have no clue what your body really is. You've witnessed its impermanence through and through. And this holds even more for your emotional state, as it's fluctuating constantly!

When you are constantly triggered by the outside, you are like a punching ball. At best, you are stable for a while, but as long as those false identities exist, they can be triggered any time. That's what you call "pushing your buttons." You feel like a free human, but then you visit your parents, and no matter how old you are, you fall into a different role, and suddenly you are behaving like a child. Your behavioral patterns are so deeply, deeply engrained in you.

As you come to understand this mechanism, you can also see all the patterns you have created, either to be validated, to get a pat on the shoulder, an appreciative look, or to avoid being rejected. This is what dictates your daily life. The patterns say, "Go there, this is nice, this is good, this is pleasant," or "Don't go there," so you can avoid whatever you rate as unpleasant.

Well, this is the human game that needed to be experienced. Thus, it is not about despising it. It *had* to be that way. You had to take on the false identities so that at some point you could really know – deep from within – *that all identification is false,* is bogus, and is make believe. It's not real!

Now you are at that point! Because you've understood that, you can also realize that all those stained glass windows that dictate your life and your life experiences are held in place *by you!* Nobody else does it for you. *It is you!* They come from *your* beliefs, *you* validate them, and *you* believe them to be real. *This is all you!*

This should be a great relief, because since it is you who is forcing this upon you, and not some higher power, *you can undo it!*

You can undo it, or you can play along with it consciously. You can consciously maintain a facade, but whatever happens to that facade, you no longer take personally. You might experience stimuli, you might interact with a client, but whatever happens does not affect you in depth. Your facade is now only a role that you consciously play. You no longer need any confirmation.

In the metaphor that we experience here in the imagination, I mentioned this spotlight. Light radiates from it and shines onto the various windows; shining through them, bringing them to life. Now, what would you say is "you" in this setup? Are you the spotlight? Are you the light? We already know you are not the windows, but then... you *make* them. What is "you," what could you identify with?

*

Now, there are no individual parts here for you to identify with, because it's all you. *All of this is you!* The spotlight, the light, all the false identities, all of this is you. That's the dream of being a human, and *it is you dreaming it.* This is the content of your dream. It is your consciousness.

Incarnating, being in flesh, makes you believe so deeply that you are *not* all of it, but that you are merely a part of it – even though with your scientific mind you do know that you cannot isolate your body from what is apparently "not your body," because everything is interconnected. Even though you know it, you still unconsciously believe that you are a body, and you hold on to certain emotional states and your false identities. You cling to them.

Why is that? Why do you cling to them?

It's simple. The price for identification is the fear of death! If everything that you believe you are vanishes, the fear of being extinguished, of falling into the void, of being nothing, of being wiped out comes to the surface. The typical humans cannot stand that fear. They run away. They hear this, they ponder this, they nod their heads, and they go back to daily life – but they don't act on it.

Therefore, it's important to go slowly with bringing all of what we have discussed today into true experience. Right now, you experience the truth of it, but the decomposing of all of your false identities is difficult, for fear will come up. So, play with it. Be playful. Do not rush.

Cultivate the awareness, but do not try to crush or suppress your false identities. It doesn't work, it never worked, and it will never work! It's your awareness, and stopping to take things personally that will work. For what could be personal for your pure consciousness? What could be personal?

It is all your interpretation and you are free to interpret as you like.

This is certainly not for everybody, and it is not meant for everybody. Be very honest with yourself. How far do you truly want to go? Go slow with it. Get adjusted to the truth of it, to the broadness of it, to the impact.

In order to go this way, you need to replace the belief in what you are with the truth about who you are. This truth does not come from separation, no. It comes from true reality, and in the moments of your enlightenment, you will feel that truth. You can ground it within you, and you know that nothing, nothing, nothing, can affect you.

Nothing can affect you in true reality. Oh sure, you might die in the physical dream, and sooner or later you will, just as all your cells are dying constantly. So what? It's not likely that you die right now. You wouldn't want to force it, though. Rather, when you become more aware, you see more potentials, and that includes the unpleasant ones. That's why you will typically have fewer accidents, simply because you are more aware. Life becomes much easier.

Without an insight into true reality, this understanding of false identities can become a source of deep frustration, for what would you do with your life? If you are a materialist, you cannot really deny what I have just said. But then, what would you do? "Squeeze everything out of the moment," they say. "Enjoy life to its utmost limits." Sounds wonderful, but you did that for eons, until you felt, "No more. I'm just repeating the same old story" and then you incarnated.

Now, shift your perspective. See your sphere of stained glass windows from the outside and be with me, outside of your human vessel, outside of your human physical and emotional body.

*

You are exactly at the right time, at the right place. Right now, you see that you can just shift out of human sphere. Oh sure, when you go back to human-only mode, it's still difficult. But, now you know the mechanics, you know the way out. And you know that you do not need to rush anything.

I'd like to remind you of the homework challenge. Cultivate your awareness every morning after you wake up. Thirty minutes. And the specific challenge here is to really cultivate your awareness, and not try to relive what we just did. You can do this all the rest of your day, but while you cultivate your awareness, be very vigilant about what goes on in your physical body, and how the various stimuli trigger emotions. As you become aware of it, let it go. You just let it go.

And then, a couple of times a day, you just stop and become aware of your inner emotional state. You might pinpoint names for some false identities that are currently active – it's not necessary, but you might. "Oh, here he or she is again!" And you interrupt the cooperation; just interrupt it. "Enough! I see you, but I do not compromise anymore on the emotions you want to impose on me."

Next week, we will speak about cultivating the light body. This will be another way to go beyond the emotional body. So this week, in a way, was a preparation. Next week, we will go one step further with cultivating the light body.

I'm looking forward to it! I will see you next week, here at this gathering, and whenever you call me in.

I am Althar, the Crystal Dragon. Thank you.

*

Joachim: One or two are still in outer space, and that is fine.

Althar said he would pick three of you to give a three minute speech of the highest wisdom, but this wasn't meant seriously; unless you insist, and raise your hand, and say, "Give me those three minutes!" If you do, don't forget to unmute yourself. Either that, or you are the wise guy, saying that the highest wisdom means not talking at all! As you like!

Or both! You can talk without saying anything; it happens all the time.

Participant 1: My wife tells me that frequently!

Joachim: Oops!

Are there any remarks, or questions to share? Do not hold back.

Participant 2: Well I would like to contribute something tonight. I'm in a very interesting setup here. I'm in my girlfriend's home, who is in the final stages of this earthly experience.

It's like a circus, that's all I can say.

I've been grasping quarter of hours just to cultivate the awareness, and I must say it's helped me tremendously, to always remind myself to step out and just be in the observing position, instead of getting into this tornado of emotions and demands and so forth. So, I'm just expressing my gratitude for this class with everybody, thank you.

Joachim: And you know, it can really be a great help for those who are departing to just be with them, without much talking. Just be in silence, join in silence, for then the false identities are just moving away. Typically, the one dying is held back by those who are grieving. But they have to depart anyway, so the grieving is not a helpful. So, if there is someone in clarity, and – depending on the person who is dying – someone who can say, "Well, I can be with you, if you so choose, even after you have departed. For in spirit, you'll still be there, and we can feel each other," this can be of a tremendous help.

But of course you have to weigh whether you can talk about this. Concerning the others who are all around, if they feel there is someone who is not in drama mode, who is just accepting the facts of life, ah, then things become easier even for them.

Participant 2: Yes they do. It's quite amazing because we also do night shifts and when it was my turn, I laid down after my shift; I wanted to go to sleep because my body was tired, and I couldn't. And then she popped up in my mind and said, "Show me how to do it, what's this, come on take my hand and show me." So, in the end I just went up again, and did another shift, and just sat with her, and she was so peaceful. It was really truly amazing, and all the people who come, they feel this. They don't know what it is, but they feel it.

Joachim: And it's the simplest thing: just be. It's the natural thing. Yes, that's a tremendous blessing. This is also a state where many people are receptive. Well, not all of course, but some are. They feel, "Oh, here is a huge change going on." Most people don't face death too often, but then they realize, there is a different way to approach life – even if you are dying you can approach life somehow. And there are big lessons to be learned, with everybody involved. It's always a good turning point, a chance for a turning point.

Participant 2: Thank you.

Participant 1: Share with me again the three minute assignment, or the three minute invitation?

Joachim: This was to show the workings of the emotional body. I said three of you would be picked to give a three minute speech about your highest wisdom. Then, see what's coming up within you on an emotional level.

Participant 1: Okay, may I?

Joachim: Sure, start. Oh, wait. Let me start my stopwatch first. Now it's your turn! Three minutes!

(*laughter*)

Participant 1: By the way, I apologize for being late on the scene; I was getting the time zone change. I missed it.

Joachim: (*chuckles*) This was the first minute!

Participant 1: I am joyfully and gratefully

playing in this body, in a way that this whole life-time has been very different than that. I delight in watching this marvelous, amazing, goofy, goofy world happen. I have developed the ability to understand and feel the idea of there being a new world; new earths, available; and I'm able to go there as I choose, to the new earths. I realize, capital R, I Realize, the grace and ease of creating, of intention immediately becoming my home, or whatever I choose to put together. I understand the possibility of that, I understand the logic, I understand the *ofcourseness* of how it happens instantaneously, how energy comes together sourced within me to become my whatever. I'm free of any agenda about love. I love, so hi, I love you, and it's simple, and it's the only way to go. That's it.

Joachim: Thank you.

Participant 1: The only things that came up for me emotionally were simply the excitement, the enthusiasm, or the joy. I feel it on new levels, and so, you're welcome, and thank you. I feel it on new levels that have been developing for some time, and have become more clearly articulated in the last week or so. I think my experience with us is a contribution to that.

Joachim: Thank you.

Participant 1: You're welcome, thank you very much.

Joachim: I have a question. Is there anybody

who would like to share any specific... expectations is the wrong term... desires for this program, what you want specifically out of this, or are you all so open, you'll just see what comes?

Participant 2: I think that's best.

Joachim: Yes it's best to be open for sure, but sometimes you are aware of something within you that you cannot put your finger on, and maybe we can address it, or maybe not, I'm just curious.

Participant 1: There's something I can share there.

Joachim: Sure.

Participant 1: What motivated me to join was reading the first five Althar books. That's the only thing I have ever done so sequentially, and as soon as I put down the fifth book, I picked up the first one again, and reread all five again. When I was a young lad, a few weeks before I almost killed myself, my question was, how does this all work? And I felt it articulated it in the five volumes clearer than anything I'd ever experienced, and I decided there was nothing else I would ever have to read again! And I was mistaken.

This program to me was simply about deepening my experience of how it all works, not only being a part of it – that was a bonus – I just wanted to know how.

Joachim: Yes, and it's actually really about bringing it to life. It's one thing to have the understanding. I think that's the prerequisite for being able to let go of most of the things, but then also to experience it. Otherwise, it's just another, I wouldn't say theory, maybe it's more than a theory, but it's up there in the mental, and not really real. This is what this program is all about, bringing it to life and validating it on your own.

Participant 1: Yes. Knowing something in my belly is my criteria; I knew that with the first book, "Althar – The Crystal Dragon." After the first chapter or whatever, I was like, okay.

Participant 2: For me it's still a paradox within… functioning in this reality, especially through this experience that I've created for myself. It becomes so much more a paradox, and how am I going to function from now on, knowing and being in this vastness? That's the only way I can put it. That might be a question that I would like to play with.

Joachim: The answer is "playful." But how to get there? (*chuckles*) Exist playfully.

Participant 3: I've been doing this for eleven months, reading all the books over and over again, and I still move I guess in my emotional body with some expectations that I'll get to this stage that Althar was talking in the books about, these, I don't know what he says, advanced senses, like beyond human senses, but not to seek them as goals. I kind of get that, but it's been difficult not to have other ideas just come in. The doctors say I have glaucoma and I notice some-times I might be doing the Light Body exercise, and I notice part of me is testing my eyes, like I'm still not seeing as good or something, so I guess I'm running these expectations. Not very often, but they pop up. I don't know if you want to speak to that or not.

Joachim: That's absolutely normal. I would say you are lying to yourself if you say you wouldn't expect something. Sometimes, you want to prove yourself, doing some "magic light" healing. Does it work or not? You cannot really deny that you try it. But the moment you realize it, let it go. It doesn't bring you any further or any faster to the point where healing might happen.

But always be honest with yourself. When you realize, "Oh, there is this part of me that wants to prove I am right or I am wrong, or I am not good enough…" The moment you notice it, stop com-promising! Do not cooperate anymore with that, and go back to the basics. But do not deny that you were trying. I think it's absolutely normal, and it's the most normal thing for a human with your condition to do this. Always, always you have learned that in order to get something you have to do something, and then you check if you have it already or not. But as soon as you realize that you are following these thought patterns, let them go. Then it goes much faster.

Participant 3: Thank you.

Participant 4: I'm wondering if anyone else has felt this. Like after the first session that I was in, not on this series, but a couple before, I had this feeling that: it's gone, it's over; the game. Does that make sense?

Joachim: Yes, absolutely.

Participant 4: Does anyone else have that feeling? And now I need to decide how I want to play.

Joachim: Game over, but still in the game!

Participant 4: The dream. Has anyone else felt like that; like you actually have a choice?

(laughter)

Cool, cool, it's not just me.

Joachim: It's always so important to stay honest with yourself and not to create new illusions. This is a special state where you just know that you know. Then, when you go back to the human perspective, it's not as easy as you would like it to be, but it's getting easier. And without staring at your watch, and without any pushing, well it truly becomes easier.

There is a huge latency in physicality. It reflects you, but it takes a while until it does, for it is *so* slow. You have to be aware of that, and then you can continue the game.

What I always say is: The easiest way to change your reality is to change what you create within yourself. How do you rate whatever comes to you? Because it's the feelings you have that define your life.

If you are the master of your feelings, then it doesn't matter what is going on outside. On the other hand, the more you free yourself, the more your freedom is mirrored to you, and it becomes even easier. So it's the opposite of a vicious circle! It goes up and up, it gets easier and easier.

On the other hand, if you get depressed it gets more and more difficult every day. That's separation!

Participant 4: That's awesome! Thank you. Thanks everybody.

Participant 1: Sounds more like a torus than anything else.

I'm reading to two friends of mine, actually clients, from *The New Magi*, we read on Sunday every morning on the phone, and we just finished chapter 9. Althar speaks of blueprints, and that's it. To me, it's like, whoa, let me get out my mind maps, let me create a blueprint, presuming myself in the state of full consciousness and embodied ascension. Okay, what does my life look like, which is how I was able to give you the response earlier I gave you, because I did a mind map on it just over the last few days. That word blueprint. Okay, I can do a blueprint; my male brain can do a blueprint.

Joachim: To be precise here, you want a blueprint to function within separation, within this dream. You don't want a blueprint for existing beyond separation, for then you are beyond blueprints. But for living the paradox, you do need a new blueprint. Everybody believes in the reality of his body, in his emotional state, in his mind and the reality of what he understands, the concepts. Yeah, but that's *so* yesterday.

We need a blueprint that allows us to be beyond. This is established as we go and therefore Althar – and I feel this so strongly – always emphasizes: This is not just about you!

As we move along here, as we open up to this, it becomes easier for everybody else, for there is a new blueprint created. And getting in resonance with something that already exists makes it obviously easier to accomplish. It's like learning math. Two thousand years ago, the Greeks were fumbling with circles and triangles. Now you learn this in elementary school. But back then, geometry was a big challenge. But learning something that exists already is easy.

Same here; if there are, say, "standards" who did it, kind of role models, then it's much easier to, well, play that role, and even go beyond it. And that's what we are doing. So, Althar also emphasizes it is actually not really important if you become a fully embodied ascended being in this lifetime. It'd be great for you, but it's not the point. It's really not the point. It's about moments of enlightenment. And this is a great relief; it's a great adventure anyway, and, well, if you check out before fully realizing embodied ascension, you can still join in suchness. It might be a bit different, but not that different.

Participant 5: When that game is over, and you feel that let go, there is still this space of what I experience as kind of a void, where that new blueprint hasn't arrived, and we're creating it as we go, but it also does feel a little bit, I don't know, discombobulated, and you don't know who you are; there's no identity. I would like just to connect in that space; I can find it difficult sometimes; being in my non-humanness, or what to call myself from there, and then how to function from that state of no identity, and moving forward from that place.

Joachim: I would say I know that place very well, if not to say for decades; arriving in the blackness or "nothingness." It wasn't really scary for me. Not really, not ever. But, I feel it's an in-between zone. It's not like this reality, and it's not like the beyond, it's somewhere in-between. At any rate, it was always very relaxing to be in that state. Well, there is not much going on, you're just there. The physical body can truly relax and rejuvenate while you are in this state. But again, there is no way of pushing you beyond that state, for if you tried, you just create something else: a new mirror; this may become a new experience in some way, but it's certainly not the way out.

What has happened in my case? I no longer find myself there very often. That state is available to me, but I'm just not ending up there anymore. I don't really know why. It changed, and now I'm in the opposite state. It's not dark, it's absolutely light. In a way it's the same, there is

71

not much to perceive, it's just brightness, but it's totally full. It's the opposite of absence, it's the fullness.

Well, both are interesting states, but I would say the fullness relates more to true reality, and the absence is more the in between zone where the consciousness that is still woven into physicality realizes, "Oh, I still exist even though there is nothing that validates me." This is an odd state.

Without any agenda to change it, it will change sooner or later. If not, so be it!

The most important thing is not to cultivate the wish to be at another place than you are right now, no matter where that is. You are not wishing to go anywhere. You can stop interacting or stop compromising with what comes to you and this brings you to another state or mental space. But it's not that you run there in any way. It's by not-doing, by not-wanting, that you arrive there.

It's coming back to the natural state. I repeat it over and over, and this is when things just fall into place and even the questions and answers fall apart, for they don't play any role anymore.

Participant 2: I call it the void.

Joachim: Yes, that's the common term and most people who start with true meditation, experience it. A single moment without reflections, and they are so shocked that they run away! "I need to distract myself, so I can have a reflection of myself. Then I know that I exist. I never want to have anything to do with meditation again."

Another common phrase is, "It didn't work for me. I tried it, but it didn't work for me." Sure, it doesn't work, there's nothing that could "work!"

Good. Thank you for being here – see you next week!

3. Fundamentals of Cultivating the Light Body

Let's start with cultivating the awareness. As always, I repeat the essentials of this because it is of utmost importance that you truly get its essence.

First, take on a royal posture! You are sitting upright. A good helper for this is if you imagine there was a thread at your crown pulling you upward. You're pulled upward, so everything in your body stretches, the whole body stretches. Your backbone stretches, the neck stretches. If you are pulled up from the top of your head, then your chin automatically goes a bit inwards, which stretches the neck and allows for a good energy flow. Also, when you stretch, you can relax and drop everything else along that stretch. You can drop your shoulders, even your belly; just give all that over to gravity.

Then, if you are in a totally upright position, you do not need any muscle force to keep it. You can just sit upright for eternity! It's a very comfortable position to start with and to cultivate the awareness.

The eyes are three quarters closed, the vision is about forty five degrees downward without you focusing on anything; the energy of the glance goes within.

Your fingers are closed. You might put your hands together or just lay them on your legs separately. But if you can, it is good to put one hand into the other, that way you have a closed loop in your energy cycles.

The mouth is closed. The tongue is touching the back side of your upper teeth. You breathe through the nose, in and out.

I repeat that with cultivating the awareness we do not want to achieve something, like a deep state of relaxation, and not even a deep state of awareness, no. It's just becoming aware in the moment. You revert to your natural state. Depending on your form of the day, this might be very easy one day, and very difficult on another. But you just do not care! You just observe, and whatever comes, whatever you feel within, you just take notice, and do not associate anything with it. You do not judge it, do not go into an inner movie and replay it, no. You just let it go the moment you become aware of it. Good.

Now become aware of your feet. Place the awareness in both of your feet.

As you do, your breath continues to come naturally, in and out.

Now include both of your legs in their entirety in your awareness.

Now feel all the body weight as it presses on your buttocks.

Become aware of both of your hands.

As you become aware of your hands, you realize how they relax. How they stop holding on to anything.

Become aware of your lower arms.

And now include your belly. Feel how it moves as you breathe.

Now feel your diaphragm. Just observe it. It's oftentimes difficult to really relax the breathing muscles, the diaphragm, everything that's connected with breathing. Breathing means living. Now, there is a fear to living for most humans, so there are blockages everywhere, tiny blockages. As you place your awareness in these regions, they can relax; the blockages melt away. The breathing becomes natural, unhindered. The energy flows, vitality comes back. It's all related to breathing.

Once again, stretch your backbone, for even if you did it in the beginning, you will notice that your posture changes all the time, constantly, with every breath you take your posture changes. You tend to fall back into the body posture that you have throughout the day, so come back to this royal position, to this upright position, the position of clarity.

Now feel your heart region, at the center of your chest. The heart is a miracle. It goes on and on and on. Nobody really knows why it beats, or when it first starts beating. As you become aware of the heart, you can feel it beating. You might even feel the blood rushing through your ears. And as you become aware of the chest region, even the heart responds. It calms down.

Now become aware of your shoulders.

Your throat.

Your lips.

You might imagine yourself becoming tiny in your awareness and walk around your lips, a full circle; feel every tiny muscle. Feel how these muscles react to your emotions, how they reflect your emotions to others.

Now feel specifically the skin on the area below your nose and above your upper lip. It's a highly sensitive region. You can zoom in here, and take note of even the slightest breath.

Now feel the tip of your nose.

Now feel your eyes. They are still not fully closed, but a little bit open. It's so much easier to stay aware, to stay awake, if the eyes are just a little bit open.

Now feel your ears, both of your ears.

From your ears, go into the interior of your skull. Place your awareness there.

Now feel the skin of your head, your forehead, and your crown.

The human language is a very difficult thing; we have to use expressions like, "Place your awareness here or there" and it gives the impression that you take something and bring it there. Or like you focus onto something by holding a magnifying glass on a certain point or area of your body.

But in essence, the awareness is already there.

It's kind of like standing on solid ground and looking for water. You would start digging into the earth, and then suddenly, if you dug deep enough, the water would flow into the hole. So the water was there all along, everywhere, you just couldn't see it.

It's the same with the awareness. The awareness is everywhere, but you just don't realize it, because you are usually focused on very few sensory inputs. So, when I say, "Become aware of your feet" – well, just become aware of the awareness that is already in your feet. The awareness is everywhere!

It's separation that makes one believe that there is a boundary around oneself, and therefore awareness is also limited.

Now become aware of your blood, everywhere in your body, as it pumps through your veins, through your arteries, and through your heart.

Become aware of that flow, the pressure, the pumping; all the movement.

Interesting, your blood moves all the time, yet your awareness doesn't move. It doesn't move at all. So you might say, the blood moves within your awareness.

Now extend your awareness beyond the body, like 20 cm, or 30 cm, or 40 cm around your body. Include that area in your awareness.

The awareness penetrates your entire body. It's all around you, it's in your body. At some point it feels like your body is "held" in some way by your awareness. It's like your body is floating in it.

You might feel a difference between the awareness which is light, without any weight, and the body which is very dense; gravity is constantly pulling at it and the muscles working to keep the body upright.

But your awareness is just there, without any effort.

Now hold the awareness. I will be quiet for a few minutes. Whenever you feel distracted, whenever you are pulled away by thoughts, stimuli from the outside, noises, emotions, feelings, thoughts… whenever you notice that, just come back. Just come back to the pure awareness.

This is truly a coming back to the natural state on the level of the body. Just being; being present, being available.

*

Good, we will now play the Althar theme song, and bring him in. Then we will have some experiences with the fundamentals of the Light Body Exercise.

(*Music plays*)

*

I am Althar, the Crystal Dragon.

What a delight it is for me to be with you once again in this third gathering of the Althar Intense Online Program.

Today, I did not come in alone, but with a whole swarm of dragons, which overwhelmed Joachim a little bit! I apologize for that, but still, here we are! A whole swarm of dragons, and guess what? These dragons belong to you! There is one for every one of you. Your dragon came with me today, for we are going to discuss what I call "Cultivating the Light Body." I say it's the highest wisdom you might encounter in your human life; the highest wisdom. For it explains the "Why" of separation, the "How" of separation, and also how to get beyond it.

There is always, always, always a problem with the highest wisdom; it has been that way for ages: The highest wisdom is by its very nature of utmost simplicity, utmost simplicity, and that is precisely why it is so easily rejected by the humans! They hear it and nod their heads, but they do not get the profundity. They try it once, but they lack the true understanding, so they dismiss it and seek something else. They try the next thing that comes along.

This is the very reason why in almost every tradition it has taken decades for a disciple or an adept to be initiated. So that by then, he was open enough, willing enough and capable to receive the highest wisdom and to accept it, without rejecting it – full of trust, full of inner knowingness.

Cultivating the light body falls exactly into this category. I could tell you the fundamentals in three sentences – and I will – but then it's up to you to apply it, to realize its depth – to bring it into your life and make it an experienced reality.

Sometimes I use the term "Light Body Exercise," for it's not as bulky as "Cultivating the Light Body," but even though it sounds like an exercise, it is not! It is just not.

It is coming back to your natural state. And your natural state is anything but being incarnated in human form, human flesh, and human bones.

It's coming back to your natural state! And this is your birthright! It's your birthright. You don't have to earn it, but you have to apply it.

We try to go into the essence of this exercise very slowly so that you can really experience the various details and aspects of it. We will play some music to enhance the experience, for the music is always a good helper to let go of the mind and to go deep, deep into the feelings.

(Music plays)

In order to start, join with your dragon aspect! Just shift your awareness. The dragon is right here with me, you could say in a special dimension, outside of human mass consciousness, but still close to your human aspect.

So, just do it, become aware of the human aspect of you. Then expand your awareness to include your dragon aspect.

You might feel the lightness of your dragon aspect; similar to what you felt just before as you cultivated your awareness. The dragon aspect has a form of your liking. It can take on the shape of a dragon, but it doesn't have to.

Now, from your dragon aspect, have a look at your human aspect. Since we are beyond time, you can see your life before you as in an unwound filmstrip. You can go back and forth in this special thread of time that your human acted out and experienced.

Find a moment in your thread of time when you decided to go for a walk in nature.

It was a very simple decision, no major turning point, nothing special. But *why* did you decide to take that walk in nature? What was the motivation to do that?

Maybe you wanted to feel the fresh air; feel the sun on your skin, feel the communion with nature itself. You wanted to feel the exercise of the body, or you wanted to feel being all on your own, without the usual struggles around you

The crucial word here is "feel." You desired to have certain feelings. Ultimately, you set out on that walk in nature, because you expected to feel certain feelings as a result. Actually, this is the core reason why a human, and indeed any entity within separation, does anything at all:

The human wants to experience certain feelings!

That is the major motivational factor! You can set aside for a moment all activities that you do for your bare survival. However, if you look precisely, even these are connected to feelings. You want to feel the breath in the lungs, so you breathe. You want to feel warmth, otherwise you would die of cold. You want to have the feeling of living. Even bare survival is thus connected to feelings. Yes, there might be a different pressure, because you want to survive, but in the end it's the feelings that drive you. If it wasn't for the feelings, you would just die. You wouldn't even notice that you need to breathe. You wouldn't even notice that your body is getting too cold.

Contemporary humans in the western hemisphere usually don't have to take too much care for their bare survival. Mostly everything they do is because they *can* do it, or they assume they *have* to do it. But it's always, always the feelings that they expect; either at the end of the activity or while they do it.

So, have a look at your thread of time that you see in front of you. Look at all the activities you did in, say, the last week. What motivated you to do something? What feelings did you expect to experience in each case? Would you have done any of it if it wasn't about experiencing feelings?

*

I said the dragon is a bridge in consciousness, and in our first session, we experienced that. We connected this bridge with pure consciousness, became aware of the pure consciousness that you are. From a human perspective, there is a feeling associated with pure consciousness. I call this feeling bliss. You can use any other name, but for the sake of our discussion, I will use the term bliss. By bliss I mean the combination of all pleasant feelings a human might have: love, beauty, clarity, safety, you name it.

It's like the white light that contains all colors, that is bliss! You can connect to that. Feel it right now as you sit here in your dragon aspect. Bliss is right here.

Now you can go to the other end of the spectrum. Become aware again of your human aspect, your human body.

Where are these pleasant feelings? Where is the bliss? Where has it gone? At one end of the spectrum, you feel the absolute lightness and bliss, and at the other end, you feel the density and the absence of bliss.

This effect is based on a very simple principle: when you go into greater densities, some of the bliss is veiled. This is the effect of density; it veils parts of you, so that you have to cope with what is left! That's what happens when you go into density, and humans live in the utmost density.

In the core series, we had discussions about how that took place. It was a compression, conducted by a group called Uru. And compression was necessary, for consciousness and matter do not really work well together. You had to come to the belief that "I am a body," and therefore we had to apply this huge compression.

I used the metaphor of a reverse atomic explosion for describing the intensity of the compression. All of you know an atomic explosion and all of you have seen its mushroom cloud. It's a huge, huge energy phenomenon. Now imagine the energy you would need if you wanted to reverse such an explosion. You want to take the mushroom cloud and compress it back to where it came from. And then you even do this multiple times. Not just once, but a couple of times, a series. That's how you got from pure consciousness into the density of the human realm. And as you were compressed, the veiling set in.

The humans might be the only entities in all of creation that have more or less totally forgotten where they came from – because of the veiling resulting from the compression. It's so dense for a human, so veiled, that the true self, pure consciousness, is just out of the human's sight, out of feeling.

But at this moment, you are connected to your dragon aspect. You've lived lifetimes and lifetimes and lifetimes and you know what it means not to know where you come from. Yes, you had some spontaneous remembrances, but you had no proof of their validity, no direct experiences. But now you are here! You can bridge from pure consciousness to your humanness; from the light to the utmost density.

But in general, what happens when you suddenly find yourself in such extreme density? Even though you have forgotten where you came from, you feel the lack of bliss. In general terms, you feel the lack of certain feelings! They are just not there! So what do you do? What do you do?

You try to compensate for them. But you are in separation and you believe that you are a body. You believe that separation is real, so whatever you do, you end up going outside of yourself. You try to create certain circumstances, so that they trigger in you a certain feeling. This is how an entity thinks that believes separation is real. "I have a feeling... oh that must have been triggered from the outside! There was an outside stimulus for the feeling."

You hear beautiful music, and you say, "Oh, the music is beautiful." You see a beautiful sunset, and you say, "Well, the sunset is beautiful." But it is *not* the object or the phenomenon that is beautiful, this is merely an interpretation of your mind! The music and sunset were *reminders* of the beauty that is already there. Reminders!

That's also the reason why different people feel differently about certain works of art. Some say a piece of music is beautiful, and others just don't like it. *How can that be if the object itself was beauty?*

But, if those people with different tastes feel beauty within themselves, then they are feeling the same beauty. It's the same beauty. It's the same, but it was triggered by different phenomena coming from the outside.

And that is what the human typically believes. He believes everything has to come from the outside, and so he thinks, "If I want to feel fulfilled, I have to constantly, constantly, constantly take care of the outside. I need the right stimuli so that I can feel what I desire. If I want a feeling of the sun on my skin, then I have to take a walk, I have to go out there. Otherwise, I don't have this feeling. I want to feel beauty, so I have to listen to beautiful music, or look at a beautiful painting. Without the painting, there is no feeling of beauty!"

But because we are in separation, there is a big problem, for the stimuli are impermanent. No matter what they are and what you do, the stimuli will decay as everything does in separation!

In one moment you feel beauty, fine, but the stimulus will disappear. The sun will go down . Well, it will rise the next day, but then maybe you have clouds. You see nothing, instead you have rain and wind. So where is the beauty then? You lack the beauty, and you cannot easily create the necessary external conditions for a beautiful sunset.

And now the false identities come into play as well... Oh, they try to replicate the true feelings with pleasant emotions that are always personal. Take the feeling of love. Love is a true feeling, but then you have the emotional love, the conditioned love. Love directed to a specific person. Well, then you have a problem, for the love you experience is conditioned by "the other," which just creates another limitation, another dependency. Yes, the other was a reminder of the pure love within, no doubt about that. But then, the feeling of love was converted and distorted by a false identity. It took it and distorted the true feeling of love to conditional love, or even just conditional acceptance. And you then settle for that as a substitute for true love.

As opposed to that, a wise one would say, "I *am* love! I do not make any distinctions. I am love, *no matter what!*"

That's beyond separation. Sure, for humans it's difficult, but still it's true, and you know it.

There is the mantra of separation: enough is not enough. You get used to the stimuli, you get used to the pieces of music you hear; you need more, you need it louder. You need more TV channels; everything needs to be bigger, bigger, and bigger. More, more, more – it doesn't suffice any more. This is also a desensitizing effect. What triggered you once will not be enough tomorrow, so you have to intensify it or make it "better."

You do whatever you do, because you want to experience feelings. Ideally, true feelings, and if that does not work, you go for replacements with emotions created by your false identities.

But what if every feeling you could ever desire was already there? Like the awareness, which is already there? What if? Oh, it doesn't mean you wouldn't go on a walk in nature any more, but it means you do it as a free human, just to enjoy it. And why not experience sun on your skin and the fresh air in your lungs, if you can? But as far as the feelings are concerned, they are already within, and you know it, and you can become aware of them whenever you like.

So, here we have the deepest truth. That's true wisdom, for it is a wisdom that enables you to go beyond separation.

Here is a diagnosis of your current state: You do what you do to experience feelings. Within the density, within the veiling, you have the belief in separation. Therefore, you go to the apparent outside to stimulate the feelings that you lack, whether in the form of emotions or sometimes in the form of true feelings. And you continue, and you continue, and you continue doing that, for separation is inherently impermanent. Thus you will never arrive at true satisfaction and true fulfillment.

Now, the diagnosis is important in order to apply the right therapy. And this is available to you at any time and especially now. Right now, you are connected to the bliss, and there is no way the bliss could ever go away, for how could you cut anything out of pure consciousness when there is no separation?

The various feelings that the human desires are still there. They are just veiled, but they are still there. It's like the awareness in your body. When was the last time you were aware of your feet other than in these last Sundays when we were cultivating the awareness? It might have been quite a while ago, but the awareness is already there, you just have to apply it.

Since you have already made so much progress in loosening your belief in the reality of separation, the veil is getting thinner and thinner for you. Sometimes, it opens up completely so that *you know that you know*, and sometimes it's just a little bit of light shining through. However, the feelings are already there and you can become aware of them. That is what the Light Body Exercise is about.

Now we have the diagnosis, and we have the therapy. We know we can become aware of any feeling we desire, without requiring any outer stimulus.

It's so simple! It is so simple that it can be easily dismissed, and that would be a great pity.

In the Light Body Exercise, we address the three major layers of your human experience: the mental layer, the emotional layer, and the physical layer. And on each of these layers, there is one predominant feeling that is lacking.

On the mental layer, you lack clarity and try to compensate for it with control.

On the emotional layer, you lack love. You try to compensate for it with personal love or conditional acceptance.

Then we have the layer of the physical, and here you lack safety. Actually, you cannot compensate for the lack of safety, no matter what you do, and you know that! You know that! The lack of safety is always with you. You know that your body will die, so how could you ever compensate for that? Oh, you can suppress this knowingness, you can push it into the future, you can deny it, you can lie to yourself – but of course, you don't do that, because you have already come so far on your path. You are fully aware of your impending death. Also, your cells know it and the body itself knows.

In essence, safety is a question of survival, and the same holds for the emotional body. There we have also a question of survival. Each false identity wants to survive. That's why there are all the struggles in the world, all the friction. The false identities are crashing into each other, wanting to survive, wanting to suppress the others. Well, sometimes they may work together for a while, okay, but they do know that death comes sooner or later.

The same is true with the mental body. You are fighting for your beliefs. You are fighting for your dogma. You are fighting for your memories. You *want* them to be true. Because when your beliefs die, if they dissolve, then what becomes of you? They *are* you, so you think. When a belief about yourself passes away, it is like a small death, and you fear it. Thus, humans fight for their beliefs.

Be that as it may, the core problem here is: you know your body will die and you cannot compensate for the resulting lack of safety. Well, humans try, in all sorts of ways. They try with muscles when they are younger, with knowledge, with money, with guards, with castles, with houses, with armies, with police forces; they will do anything just to protect their safety.

If safety is at stake, everything else has to stand back. Right now, during the covid pandemic, safety is number one. Everything else is irrelevant. "We have to survive!" And yet, everybody knows that with each bite you take, you could die. Some food just needs to go down the wrong tube in your throat, and that's it. Then it doesn't matter what you did to protect yourself, nor how old you are, or knowledgeable, or wise; you would still suffocate. Thus, you just cannot compensate for safety.

Still, the feeling of safety is available. It's part of the bliss. And right now, we will become aware of it. The easiest way to become aware of safety is if you first remember an unsafe situation that you might have encountered. It may have been a difficult situation in a car, in an airplane, or on a roller coaster. Or when you were swimming in the ocean and suddenly you ran out of strength and feared you wouldn't make it back to the beach. That felt unsafe.

Opposed to that, right now, in this here and now moment, everything is safe. Everything is just safe. Feel that! Feel the safety. Nothing is threatening you right now. There is enough air to breathe, and the ground is stable.

Now imagine a dimmer with which you can change the intensity of a lamp. We use such a dimmer as a helper to increase the intensity of a feeling. It works exponentially, for we are approaching bliss and that is what you need to be able to face. You have to be able to stand the intensity of pure bliss. If you would intensify the feelings within, like safety, just a little bit, it won't take you too far. So we go exponentially! Hence, whenever you turn the dimmer one notch, the safety increases tenfold.

Do not ask how that works, just allow it.

Now use your dimmer, and turn it one notch; safety times ten. It's all around you; it's within your body. Your physical body responds, your emotional body responds, your mental body responds. Here is safety. "I am safe!"

Here we encounter another paradox. I say we don't try to do anything, we do not try to push anything, yet we use this dimmer which is of course, in a way, a pushing. Well, let's call it the exception. But you have to be very careful with yourself! If you get a clear voice from within, saying "enough intensity," then, you do not push beyond that. That is the discernment you need to have. When it's getting too intense, you do not push beyond that, but as long as it is comfortable, and even a bit beyond comfortable, without blowing you away, that's fine.

So, safety; once again, turn the dimmer one notch. Now we have safety times one hundred. Become aware of that. Safety is omnipresent.

As a human, every encounter you have, you judge in terms of survival. You walk along the street and meet a dog. You instantly check: is this a threat? You walk in the park and see a gang of young people. You judge immediately: is this a threat? Can I trust them? Is my survival at stake? You do that all the time, everywhere! Is this food good to eat, or would I die if I ate it? But now there is safety, utmost safety. No dog around, and no food; just the feeling of safety.

And, if you so choose, turn the dimmer a third time, safety times ten, meaning, a thousand times the feeling of safety from where we started.

When was the last time that you felt truly safe, truly safe? That was a very, very long time ago.

In this moment you are aware of yourself as a human, as a dragon, and as a pure consciousness that you truly are and that connects everything. Right now, you can feel into the knowingness that you are unborn. *Unborn!* You have *never* been birthed! *And what is unborn cannot die!* It just cannot. Oh, you can leave the physical dream, but so what? *Unborn! How could death be a threat to the unborn?* It's a joke. It's a dog barking at the moon.

You cannot compensate for the lack of safety. As long as you believe yourself to be a physical body, you just cannot. The moment you go beyond that belief, the moment you go beyond separation, safety is a given! No stimulus required; no walls, no muscles, and no guards. Why work for it?

As you feel safe, it radiates out. It radiates all around you, not just twenty centimeters like we have spoken of an hour ago. No, it radiates out to all of existence! Even the dog that's coming close feels safety; it just feels it; everybody feels it. And even if there is somebody else threatening you, you know you don't need to take it personally. It is not about you, certainly not.

Cultivating the light body is the highest wisdom you might ever encounter, for its simplicity, and the truth it springs from. Do not dismiss it. Have trust! Try it! Try it for yourself, apply it; open up to it.

Why is it called the light *body*? Well, the moment you become aware of your bliss, the innate quality of your pure consciousness, of your true self, and have the intent to have a light body, all around you, all around your physical body, it is there. And that will be the vessel you inhabit as you stay on the planet while you go into full enlightenment.

You could do without the light body in this exercise, and just use the feelings, but here we also use the light body to prepare your new vessel, so that you can stay. The physical body mimics what is all around it, and rejoices. "I am safe now!"

We will go deeper into the Light Body Exercise in the next session, and we will also go further into it in the sessions to come, because there are many, many more levels we can dive into.

Instead of having a long discourse and dissecting everything, it's better to introduce the individual facets one by one and experience them yourself, thus transforming them into experienced wisdom.

Now I will leave you. As for the dragons who came with me – that's up to you, and up to them. They may come close to you and you may stay in the awareness of them; it's your choice.

Oh, of course, a homework reminder!

Split the half hour that you take ideally every morning. Use the first fifteen minutes for cultivating the awareness – and when I say that, I mean just that. Do not go anywhere, not into bliss state, not to a dragon. Just be aware. That is the deconditioning. And then have fifteen minutes of the Light Body Exercise. Start with safety. You might go further if you've read the books, but otherwise, go just with the feeling of safety. You will note tremendous effects on your physical body, and on your emotional body, for all the patterns that you have created on the emotional level to receive feedback and validation can dissolve, because the feeling you are seeking through them is already there. This is the easiest way to clear and simplify the emotional body.

I am Althar, the Crystal Dragon, and it was once again an honor for me to share this deepest wisdom that I am aware of with you. See you next week.

*

Joachim: So, here we are, back again. I will make sure that you can unmute yourself. So, is everybody still there? Good!

It's time for exchange, or questions, answers, or remarks.

Participant 1: I have a question. The question just popped up while Althar was speaking, and it's about, he was saying, "The body will die." But is it not so that as we are cultivating the awareness and receiving going into the bliss state, that this automatically will configure the light body, where bodily ascension is possible?

Joachim: True, yes. I said that from the perspective of the normal human who believes in separation, and who believes him or herself to be a body, and who continues to look to the outside for reflection. If that were to change, well, everything changes. But we have to be honest with ourselves, it's not that easy to change. This belief is anchored deep, deep, deep within. As you do the Light Body Exercise and turn on the intensity, you feel all that fear of death coming up.

At some point you feel – even on the cellular level – all the resistance against this letting go of the idea that *I am physical*. That comes from deep, deep within. Therefore, we do this exercise slowly and increase the intensity slowly. But it's not a one-time exercise. It takes a while, and no one can say how long it will take for any particular person.

But it's true, the body is a dream concept, and it's only as real as you believe it to be.

Participant 1: Thank you.

Participant 2: Did we program – the deep feelings, this deepness you're talking about, it's deep within, is that what you are referring to in the books as "blueprint" and did we agree to this blueprint before, and it includes all kinds of whether, its diseases or something else, and we're now changing the blueprint? Can you talk about some of that?

Joachim: These are two different things.

There are true feelings which are part of the natural state of consciousness, and a human might name that, or perceive that as bliss, which is a lofty term, but from a human perspective, it makes sense. This is beyond any blueprint, it's just a given.

And then, the blueprints determine how the various entities can experience their lives. For example, your DNA determines if you have two legs or eight, right? So this gives you the framework for your experiences. This framework also allows you to go beyond your belief in being a human. And that is what we bring into life. We create, so to speak, the blueprint for going beyond the limited human vessel!

Okay?

Participant 2: Okay. Thank you.

Joachim: You're welcome.

4. Cultivating the Light Body - Continued

Let's begin by cultivating the awareness. First, take on the royal posture, the posture of the master. You want to be the master in your physical body, the master of your emotions, your thoughts, and your feelings. So, take on that posture.

The backbone is stretched, and, as I said last time, it's very good to imagine a thin thread attached to your crown that's pulling you upwards. It's pulling you upwards, and everything else, along that verticality in your body, you can just drop. Then, when you are sitting totally upright, you need no muscles whatsoever to keep that position. It's a very relaxing position.

The eyes are three quarters closed. The glance of your eyes is in front of you, but the energy of the eyes goes within. There is no focus in your eyes.

The mouth is shut – unless you are like me, talking all the time. The tip of your tongue touches the backside of your upper teeth. You are breathing in and out through your nose. You are breathing in such a way that you do not hear yourself.

The whole point of cultivating the awareness is coming back to a natural state. Natural means not trying to achieve anything; not trying to be in any way special, improved, better, or whatever the goal might be. Instead, just let go of everything, and become aware of everything as it touches your senses.

Today we start with just observing the breath. Just being aware of how the breath comes and goes.

Just becoming aware of your breath has tremendous effects throughout your body; throughout your physical body, throughout your emotional body, and throughout your mental body.

Wherever you place your awareness, a relaxation sets in. And as the breathing relaxes, so do the emotional body, the mental body, and the physical body. You know that every emotional state is accompanied by a special type of breathing.

If you are stressed, your breath may be like this (*shallow quick breaths*), and if you are very relaxed, you don't even notice your breath.

The breath is coming in and out. You feel how your chest moves, how your belly moves.

Coming back to your breath, even in your daily life, is the easiest way to calm down immediately. The breath is always with you, always, always. If it's not, you have a problem. But as long as you're living, the breath is with you, and by becoming aware of it in a given moment, the state of your body changes immediately.

Now become aware of how your spine is changing its position as you breathe. There is always a slight movement in your backbone even if you sit upright. Normally, you are not in an upright position during the day. You are sitting at your desk, or you are working, or walking somewhere. You are not in an upright position and the muscles in your body adjust to that. So being upright, straight, feels a bit unnatural. Therefore, as you get used to this posture, you need to resist the "normal" tension of the muscles. But this changes. After a while, the muscles adjust, and then sitting upright for a long period of time is much more comfortable.

Now expand your awareness from breathing to your belly. Feel the totality of your belly, and feel how the breathing gently massages it.

Now become aware of both of your legs. Just feel their existence.

A question came up: What does it mean to be aware of something in your body? Well, you just become conscious of it. You notice what's going on there. There's no hidden knowledge here, it's not even about feelings in any way – it's just about becoming aware of what's going on.

It's about fine-tuning your awareness so that every stimulus that comes through your body comes to your awareness; and the finer your awareness is, the easier it is to let go of all the reactions, of all the chain reactions that follow a given stimulus.

So in that respect, cultivating the awareness is not spectacular. There are no dragons involved, no immediate "enlightenment" considerations. It is simply the fundamental basis for approaching enlightenment. You *have* to be the master in your house! Otherwise, if every stimulus that comes along brings you out of balance and forces you into an inner movie trip – well, you have a problem!

So, this is the fundamental practice for deconditioning yourself. The way to decondition yourself is to become aware of your conditionings and to stop acting them out! That's all! Yet, you will feel a tremendous liberation as you do it, a tremendous liberation as you are stepping out of your patterns. That's a wonderful feeling.

But these effects are byproducts! As you cultivate your awareness, you do *not* consider any of this. You just observe what is going on, and as you notice, you let go!

Now include your arms and hands in your awareness. Especially in your fingers you might sense the temperature, if it is hot or cold or warm! You might feel how all the fingers are touching each other.

Include your shoulders and your head in its entirety in your awareness. So now you have full body awareness.

Now, that you have established this focused awareness of your body, you let go of the focus, you let go even of the notion of your body.

Just be aware of what happens in and around you.

The moment you notice that you are pulled away, by your thoughts, or whatever, you just come back. First, come back to the awareness of your body, readjust your position. Take on the master position, and then you open up again to observation.

Once in a while there might be a very annoying emotion that is ever-present. Maybe when you get up from your sleep, there is already some kind of, say, anxiety in you, and you cannot put your finger on it. You don't know where it comes from. This might happen also while you are doing this non-practice of cultivating of the awareness. And as much as you want to let the annoying emotion go, it just stays.

So you might try a small trick. Because you are so used to being a human, you have a direction in your senses; you have a front and a back. However, you can energetically turn around in your body. So, even if your head, say, looks towards the north, inwardly you could look towards the south. Just try that right now. Change the direction of your awareness. Look through to the back of your head. Don't expect to see something, but feel. What is it like?

It's a bit like putting shoes on the wrong feet, but after a while it becomes totally natural. You are so flexible in your awareness and your consciousness; you can do that easily! You can also look to the left, through your left ear, for instance.

Just give it a try. Turn energetically, inwardly, into that direction and open up towards that direction.

Now look through your right ear. Again, shift your perspective.

When there is, say, an annoying emotion, then oftentimes it comes from a certain direction, say, from the back left, and you sense it there. Well, then turn into that direction. Turn towards it, and open up, without any negotiating, just opening up to the awareness of what's going on there. In a way, you are inviting the emotion. Typically, an unpleasant emotion is suppressed or pushed away. You distract yourself, so you don't notice it anymore. Then the circumstances change and the emotion is gone. But it's never *really* gone, it's just suppressed, and it will come back.

So, in a scenario like this, turn inwardly to the direction where you feel the emotion comes from. Open up to it. And then, like we do with the dimmer in the Light Body Exercise, try to increase the intensity of the emotion, even if it's unpleasant. Say, it's a fear – increase the fear! You can increase and increase it. Sometimes it might happen that you have an instant flash, a knowingness of where the fear came from. It might be the result of some incident from this lifetime, or from another lifetime, it doesn't really matter. Oftentimes, it is sufficient to acknowledge it for what it is, and let it go.

However, sometimes it just remains to be an annoying emotion. But as you increase its intensity, for instance the fear, at some point you are realizing: *It is you who is doing this to you! It is you that amplifies the fear within you.*

In a way, this is a bit ridiculous, and you notice that. And even though the annoying feeling might still be there, well, it's losing its annoyance and grip on you. Now it might dissolve, because you don't take it seriously any more.

It is important that you do not chase after stuck energies or stuck events or false identities with your awareness in, say, your emotional body. You don't do that! Everything will come to you and you are just observant. Most often, you do nothing other than observing what is going on and not associating anything with it.

In the Buddhist tradition, there is a deep understanding of the various states of consciousness, of the various so called *Samadhi* states. The Buddha has spoken at length about them. The Indians like to create all kinds of levels for everything, so they came up with eight different states of meditation, of *Samadhi*, the eighth being the deepest state beyond everything. The most important, they realized, is the one they call the fourth state, which is what we are doing right now. They realized exactly as you do in your moments of enlightenment that all those blissful Samadhi states pass away as soon as you come back to the human condition. But the fourth state, being in open awareness, allows the deconditioning! Therefore, it became their major practice. This is what heals the human, and this is what – well, healing implies the human is sick – no he is not so sick, but this allows the human to let go of all of his false beliefs, his illusions. And as he does, the higher states of consciousness become available to him.

So, I repeat: cultivating the awareness is not about feelings, not about creating anything, not about achieving anything. It's just that: cultivating the awareness. Becoming the master in your own house; becoming flexible, and from there, everything else can happen.

It's very difficult to master the higher states, say the Light Body Exercise, and bring it into your normal life, as long as your awareness is very fragile.

Good. I will play some music, and we'll bring in Althar.

*

I am Althar the Crystal Dragon, coming in once again with a whole swarm of dragons which are your dragon aspects. You might notice that even though a week has passed it is as if we have never left. And we continue just where we left off in what you call your "last week"!

So please, once again, take on your dragon aspect by becoming aware of it; just become aware of it, shift your perspective.

Come to me, sit, as a dragon, right next to me here in this wonderful dimension, which is close to the human realm, so we can still see and perceive what is going on there, yet we are also very close to what is called true reality. Become comfortable in your dragon form, whatever you choose the form to look like, and sit here right with me.

We will have a very short recap of what we said in our last gathering. As we sit here, you feel, hopefully, in a way "from behind you," the intensity of true reality, of pure consciousness. It is right here. And on the other end of the spectrum you feel your human façade, your human physical body.

We have said that as an entity goes from pure consciousness, the less dense variants of consciousness, into the deeper densities, a veiling sets in. The effect of this veiling is that the entity loses the natural ability to be aware of the bliss which is part of its natural state.

Now, if you go so deep, so, so deep that you even incarnate, then you are at the densest density possible. Thus, the veiling is extreme. In order to even get you there, we had to apply extreme measures, like the compression and the hypnosis.

From the perspective of the human incarnated body, mostly everything is veiled. All the feelings, all the true feelings that are part of bliss, are lacking somehow, or they appear to lack – for nothing can be cut out of consciousness. So, they are still there, but the veiling prohibits the human from feeling them. And what's more, the human has totally forgotten where he came from, has totally forgotten about his true self and true reality.

He just doesn't know anything, so he starts trying to find identities, trying to mirror himself in what is all around him. By doing so, he compensates for the lack of feelings. He compensates with what I call "emotions," which are always personal. In doing so, he creates all these false identities, and he fights for them. The false identities are what the human believes himself to be. The false identities, if accepted by others, provide pleasant emotions. If they are rejected by others, they provide unpleasant emotions. Everything, *everything* is about these false identities.

In essence, the human, just like every other entity in the second round of creation, has just one motivating factor: it is the desire to feel again certain feelings, to compensate for the lack of feelings that they experience. So, that is the human condition.

Now, let's continue our discourse on the Light Body Exercise. To understand the light body, we first have to have another look at the physical body. It's perfect that we are here in our dragon form, so that you can really have a deep look into your physical aspect from the outside.

The human body consists of billions and billions and billions of cells. It consists of an enormous amount of interconnected beliefs, each mirroring itself. As you go into your incarnation, knowingness is replaced by perception. So whatever you perceive is distorted and needs interpretation. Nothing is clear when you are in a human incarnation.

The body consists of matter and nobody knows what matter really is. Yet, it's heavy, it weighs on you, and everything is in extreme slow motion. And again, the matter mirrors you. You believe, "This body is me!" You even eat matter, to sustain your physical body.

So, the physical body of the human and of each biological life form is highly, highly complex. You might say, it's the most intricate, most complex aggregation, or formation within consciousness. It's *so* complex, and you can rightfully marvel at what separation can do. It can create such an organism. It can bring forth such a thing called a biological body. Then the human comes along with his brain, which provides a totally new dimension of experience, and then consciousness in separation even comes to believe that it exist as a separated piece of matter within separation. It's unbelievable; unbelievable, yet highly, highly complex.

Consider in contrast to that the light body. I said the light body is created on the level of your true self by just having the intent to have a light body. That's it! A single intent, versus myriads and myriads of beliefs, mirrors, and singled out intents that create the physical body. So the light body is so much simpler than the physical body. And it is so much more *you!* You! *Undistorted, pure, undiluted, you!* Just *you.*

The light body is a projection all around your physical body. The light body comes full of bliss for it is connected to your true self, which is, say, in kind of a bliss state. Because of that and because your belief in separation is loosening, it becomes much easier to become aware again of the feelings that are in the light body. For, you might say, the veil is thinning. That is the magic of the light body.

As you realize that, you do not need any outer stimulus anymore to feel a certain feeling. As you really realize this down to your bones, you free yourself! You free yourself! No need to act out any longer behavioral patterns from your false identities to gain you some acceptance or to avoid harm. That's not necessary anymore, for all is here already, in the simplicity of the light body.

In the course of what is called embodied ascension, the light body and the physical body will meld. It's important not to take that too literal, for we are deep, deep in the surreal. We said the body is not real in the first place. It's all the beliefs that hold it in place. The light body is a bit more real for it stems from just a single intent, but yet, we are here in the paradox.

So, when I say "the light body and the physical body will meld," you might see it as a simplification of your total body, a simplification. You will still have a physical experience that allows you to connect and share and experience with your fellow humans. That's the whole point in staying on the planet.

At the same time, you just *know* that you are not your physical body, but the light body, which is not really here even though it is projected here. This is what liberates you moment by moment. And when that happens, embodied ascension is realized. This is where we go.

Okay, now let's continue with the light body exercise. To do so, I will once again play some music to enhance the experience.

(Music plays)

Again, you might take on a royal posture, for what you are about to do is sacred. It is truly, truly sacred. Honor that, honor this sacredness. Last week, I said it's easy to dismiss the highest wisdom and that's the reason why in so many traditions it took the initiates years and decades until they were exposed to the highest wisdom.

There's yet another reason for this, and this reason also holds for the light body exercise: the moment you are exposed to the highest wisdom, a tremendous fear comes up. And this fear is two-fold. It's the fear of biological death that is deep down in every cell of yours, and on the level of your true self, there is the fear of being extinguished. This is the whole reason why this journey through separation took you so long.

There was always a reason not to go out of separation, and the strongest reason was this fear. Of course it does not always show itself as fear, for depending on your state, depending on who you think you are, you might prefer to accept another excuse. Like suddenly you think you know that this is not for you, or you have a very important project to finalize. So you leave everything, leave this spiritual practice. There are many, many variants of this. You might say, "This master doesn't know the truth", "He's not for me, he doesn't acknowledge me enough," or "It's too simple", but the disguise doesn't really matter. All these excuses stem from the fear of death, and the fear of being extinguished. As we do the Light Body Exercise, or better said, whenever you do the Light Body Exercise on your own and you intensify the feelings within you, this fear will come up.

So it's important that you are prepared for that. Nothing is wrong with this fear, it is absolutely normal. You are conditioned to believe that you are a human in a physical body, and your physical body, your physical vessel, is made to survive. Thus, once you let go of the fundamental belief in separation, of course, everything in your make-up is faced with extinction, because you are made out of separation. *Everything that you believe yourself to be is made out of separation!* So fear is natural.

On another level, there are all kinds of incidents that have happened in your life, traumatic experiences in this lifetime and other lifetimes as well as experiences on the level of society, or of the group you are living in; the tribe, the nation, the land, the family. All this is passed down through the DNA and blueprints, through your socialization and upbringing. *All this is within you.* And as you bring in the light of pure consciousness, it is highlighted, it is exposed, and you will feel it.

These remembrances are all buried deep down in the unconscious. You never notice them unless they are triggered, and you do not want them to be triggered, so you are always finding ways to circumvent that. But as you allow the light of pure consciousness to shine throughout all the layers of your existence, wow, you *will* notice them. They cannot hide. And because of that, you will have all kinds of feelings, emotions, and flashbacks. All of that is absolutely normal and natural. The only point I want to make here is: be aware of that. It's important that you know that this will happen. This is nothing special, nothing that is happening only to you. But you have to ask yourself, "Can I stand this intensity?" And if it's too much, you reduce the intensity a little bit or come back at a later time.

Do not dismiss this highest practice, this most simple practice, when sooner or later you face your fears and all those hidden unconscious incidents. They will surface, because you cannot bring them with you beyond separation. They are anchoring you here in the human experience, in this physical experience.

Also, you might feel tremendous surges of power, for you have an animal nature deep down within you. Your biology had to survive by eating other animals, by killing and hunting. And whenever you were successful, there was a tremendous surge of power within you. This might surface again , and you might want to run out to do "the next great thing" in your life – maybe a long term project, for you are so full of energy! Well, you might do that. But it would be better to let that go, and become aware of that enormous amount of energy within. Integrate it! Allow it to be with you without acting on it!

Actually, this is where many, many have failed. They thought they had become the great magicians, and they went back into separation to act it out; to become famous, rich, honored. Don't go there! However, it's your choice. I'll be here anyway if you come back in a few dozen lifetimes. But there is no need to play the magician. Actually, you already did! You've done all those tricks, you had all those specific lifetimes, those experiences; why go there again? If you want the feeling of being honored, well, just become aware of it.

So, let's start with safety once again. Feel safety. Become aware of the safety that is already present within your light body. You see, the true self of you is in communion with you. It supports you, and holds the intent of having a light body. In that respect, it is always there, but you have to become aware of it.

Right now, become aware of the safety that is contained in the light body which is all around you, and within your body. It's just safe. Right now, there is nothing to protect, nothing you could lose, nothing to fight for, and nothing threatening you.

Use the dimmer and intensify the safety by a factor of ten – one notch on your dimmer. Allow your awareness of safety to increase, as if you put a magnifying glass on that feeling. If it was about marketing, I would say, "We go quantum!" It's a quantum leap beyond your comfort zone, beyond what you would usually do. Now it's tenfold.

And as you do, the safety spreads out through your physical body; your flesh, your bones, your blood. It penetrates your emotional body, and the safety also goes directly into your mental body. But first and foremost, safety is lacking on the physical level.

Once again, use your dimmer, safety times ten. Now we have a factor of one hundred.

The physical body is afraid of death. It believes it has been born. It believes it exists in time. It believes it's a child of time. You know better.

You know that you know better.

Once again, use the dimmer. Now we have safety times one thousand.

In this intensity of safety, it appears as though the physical body gets transparent.

So, safety is the number one lacking feeling on the physical layer.

Now let's go to the emotional layer. What is lacking here is the awareness of love. Where is the love? Somehow you remember how you have been love. There was love all around. It's unnatural that love is lacking and to have to do something to get it, but you learned that you had to do something to get it as a physical being. Your mother was so much nicer to you when you were laughing instead of crying. So you learned that you better laugh and smile.

The replacement for love is conditional acceptance. Love is hard to get, but conditional acceptance – that is in the reach of the human. Thus, you behave in a certain way, so that others accept you. Then you feel good. That's the compensation for love. And that's what all the false identities do, day in, day out. They make sure they get conditional acceptance, and avoid rejection, for rejection hurts.

However, of course there are moments of love. Moments of love! But moments of love are a bit like moments of enlightenment, aren't they? True love can only exist if there are no boundaries between you and the other, or between you and anything. Since each of you has already experienced a moment of enlightenment, I'm sure everybody has also experienced a moment of love. So please, remember such a moment now. It might be your first love, or an occasion with your pet, the smile of your child. There was love and you remember it. And actually, this was a reminder of the pure love that is always already there, that is just veiled.

Now you might feel your light body as a loving embrace throughout your body, every layer, every cell, every false identity, every traumatic experience, every blueprint, and every strand of DNA is embraced. There is acceptance. Total acceptance! That is what love actually is. "I can be as I am." That is the feeling of being loved – without being rejected or without the need to prove anything.

Now use your dimmer, intensify it. Love times ten.

Remember, you are safe. You are safe, and there's a feeling of love. What a combination! For as far as you can remember, each love that you experienced was accompanied by fear; the fear that "the other," or the occasion would change. And deep down within, you knew of course that everything changes all the time. So what was a moment of love then became a memory. Then it may have been changed into trust and loyalty. The moments of love, of true love, are rare, just as the moments of enlightenment are rare.

118

Look at your society and see what people do to get love, or even its substitute, conditional acceptance. It's unbelievable. Almost everything is about that. If the dictators of the world would feel unconditional love, oh, they would behave differently.

Now, once again, use your dimmer, love times ten.

That is simplification. The false identities, they are like crystals of ice and they just melt away. They are not required anymore! They have no existence in and of themselves anyway. It is *you* holding these false identities in place, and as you realize that you do not need them anymore, you take back all of your attention, and they just cease to exist.

And now a third time: love times ten with your dimmer, turn it one more notch, without holding back.

It's nurturing, do you feel that? It's like you are eating with every cell. You're taking it in. Finally, finally, there is love again. Unconditional love, not bound to time, or you behaving in a certain way.

When you do this on your own, with less talk in your ears, there might be many feelings coming up within you. Tears might flow, body parts might be shaking. Allow that for a while; but after, say, a few weeks that you do this practice, at some point you have to step out of that and just observe it. For as beautiful as these arising feelings and emotions are, the body reactions can also become a hindrance. It's so overwhelmingly beautiful and emotional that you'll have to stop it. You'll have to stop it over and over again, until your forget about the whole practice at some point. So be aware of that, be aware of that – for that is another way the hidden fear can disguise itself.

Now let's get to the mental layer. The mental layer is so interesting, for, in a way, it's not physical. Everything here happens fast, without much latency. So it's much more natural than the slow motion physical experience.

When an entity goes into density, the veiling that sets in within the mental layer causes a lack of clarity. In pure consciousness, there aren't any questions. There is not a single question, not a single doubt.

Can you imagine that? Can you imagine a moment in your life without doubt? So, when going into density, the doubt comes. Skepticism comes. Moreover, you change from knowingness to perception, and whatever you perceive is distorted. *Nothing is as it seems to be!* Everything has to be interpreted, and you can interpret it in whatever way you like. So, how can you be sure that the way you interpret it is the right way?

So, on the mental layer is the doubt – doubt of everything. To compensate for the lack of clarity, the human seeks control. The human likes to control its environment, and the more control there is, the more clarity there seems to be, for whatever is going to happen is known in advance.

Control compensates for the lack of clarity. This is obviously a great illusion, but it helps to get through the day. This desire for control – or for clarity – is what all the researchers are acting out. They want to know and model everything. They want to go deeper and deeper into the details although they know that there is no end to the details. But it keeps them distracted. It keeps them in the illusion of control.

Clarity. The easiest way to feel clarity is if you remember a point in your life where you had to make an important decision. Should I choose this or that career? Should I leave my partner or should I stay? Should I have a child? At such an important point in your life, you might have had a huge intuition, a knowingness from within that you couldn't explain. You just knew, "This is the way to go." That was a moment of clarity.

Clarity doesn't need arguments, for every argument comes from separation, it's arbitrary. The knowingness is just that, knowingness. It doesn't need support.

So, choose a moment in your life where you had such an intuition, and remember how you felt in that moment. This is the feeling of clarity.

Now, use the dimmer, and increase the clarity by a factor of ten. Clarity times ten! That in combination with safety, and love; what a feast!

I know that I know. That is clarity!

I am that I am. That is clarity!

I know without reason, without reasoning, and without any detail.

What is called the mental body is huge, it is huge! In a way, it's like a cosmos in itself. We could say that every belief is like a star shining along, trying to influence you. And you have galaxies, which are like religions – multiple beliefs on top of each other, always circling around themselves. You have swarms of asteroids, like your thoughts. Sometimes they collide with each other, or they collide with planets and stars. You can find many analogies between what you see in the cosmos and the beliefs, dogma, and convictions held in the mental body. You might say a false identity is like a black hole. It sucks everything in, even the light. It sucks it in on one side, and spits it out the other as an emotion, right into the emotional body.

As you bring clarity into this, into your personal cosmos of mental activity, everything in here can relax. You realize that everything here exists just to cut separation into ever smaller pieces; into more and more details, into right and wrong, good and bad, yesterday and tomorrow. With clarity, you don't need that any more.

Just as your physical body relaxes when you bring awareness into it, just as your emotional body can relax as you bring love into your awareness, so can the mental body relax. Your concepts, dogmas, and beliefs can relax, loosen up, and become less rigid. That is what clarity does.

I always say that nothing, nothing, nothing withstands pure consciousness. Oh, clarity is of pure consciousness. No belief can withstand clarity.

Now again, clarity times ten.

I know that I know. I know I am unborn, so death is not even a question, it's a false belief making the experience of being a human so very, very real.

I know it's not about going backwards from the deep density of being a human to the loftier densities. It is about going beyond each and every density.

So in essence, the human body is the way out, the portal, the gateless gate. But it requires letting go of the belief in death, and the fear of death, and the fear of being extinguished. For what are you if there is no mirroring of you?

Now take the dimmer once again; clarity times ten!

You're like a shining light, an entity of clarity, of love, and of safety.

As you allow these feelings, you can see or feel how all activity comes to peace. Time seems to stand still. What was important an hour ago is of no concern right now.

At this stage of the Light Body Exercise, you can add more feelings. Clarity, love, and safety are for the three main layers of your physical existence, but depending on your personal, say, structure and conditionings, other feelings might be very helpful. Like beauty. Add beauty to the feelings. Remember a moment when you felt beauty, then let go of that image, for every image and even every memory is like a stimulus. You do not need that, just become aware of beauty, of the essence of beauty. Again, take the dimmer. How beautiful is that?

Add the feeling of freedom – the feeling of being beyond any limit, any boundary, and any restriction – that doesn't mean that you fly around with your physical body. That's not the point. The point is that you know you are not your body, therefore you can fly as you like.

You might choose to add vitality, the feeling of vitality.

Now, allow all of those feelings to blend into a single feeling of bliss, into the essence of bliss.

From a didactical perspective, it's helpful to dissect bliss, for this understanding is important for your experiences and for your way out of matter. But then, there is no need to dissect bliss, just feel the bliss in its totality. It's all around you – wherever that is. It's all within you – if that even exists.

Now I invite you to shift your perspective totally into the light body and leave your physical body. It's still there, you are still connected to it, but your center of awareness becomes the light body.

Let the body know that it doesn't have to fear death, for there is no such thing. Let it be known throughout your light body, and your physical body will accept it. It will mimic the light body, for it recognizes you. Deep down in that physical body are still parts of you, clinging to the subatomic structures, believing to be of matter. And they gently, gently wake up.

Today we will not go there, for we are not in a rush, this is not a race.

Feel again the simplicity of your light body. *This is you!* Deep down within you know:

I am the living light!

I am the living light, *without any doubt!* And isn't that the living paradox? To be *in* the dream but not *of* it?

It is so simple. If you came to accept the underlying motivation for doing this exercise, if you made it your own wisdom and apply it, it has the highest potency!

This is a sacred moment, and I want you to feel that right now you are not alone. There are many others with you experiencing this in their very own way, but in the end it's all very similar. They are sharing your way. It might be difficult to talk about it, but you know you are not alone, not on this side of what is called "the veil," and surely not on the other side.

Now, slowly, slowly open your physical eyes. There is no reason to let go of the bliss, of the state you are in, for it's not a "state," It's your natural beingness. It's what you are, the living light, disguised as a human.

(Althar leaves quietly.)

*

Joachim: So, everybody back in their current disguise?

Does anybody have a remark or a question? Don't hold back.

Participant 1: I guess Althar is saying we're this living light. We are the light body, and in the book Althar says we're limitless, without boundaries, and I don't know, maybe he'll talk some more about limitlessness, because it seems like what I read in the book is we're in this transitional stage. I don't know how much people in our group have been doing the book. I've been doing it for close to a year, working on the light body cultivation exercise. Every day, sometimes multiple times a day, and using like pedal to the metal stuff, with huge numbers. Even working with infinity!

Now, I did get a bad dream when I did it four months ago with the pedal to the metal, but since then I went up gradually and now I'm up to infinity, or ten to the infinite power. How can we lose this?

I get in the book that this transitional period can be, if not dangerous, we can slip back into separation. How can we do that with like what we just did today? We are the living light, we are the light body, and we are unlimited. How can we slip back?

Joachim: *If you allow it* that is the simple answer. If you allow parts and pieces of you to try to take hold of it, you see. You might then have the feeling of being special; that you want to teach others, others come to your doorstep and they are admiring you. Then all the ego games start over again. It happens over and over again, just you look around, and it's very difficult not to fall prey to that. Now if people come and admire you, and you suggest them to do that, well, you have a difficult time ahead of you. You have to be very stable not to go there.

Apart from that, it's always separation slipping in once again, trying to get hold of some hidden aspects of you that feel "I want to show the other guys." That's a problem, the biggest hindrance, and each person will respond individually. Depending on how your life was, if you have had a position of power in your usual business life for instance, then you might be done with the issue of power. Or, it may be that you have never had a position of power, and suddenly there is a group of, say, ten people around you and you are the guy they are listening to. Then the dynamics of separation can easily pull you back. It doesn't happen usually if you are practicing on your own. But at some point you can be tempted to go out and try to manipulate or influence others – that is why you have to be so aware of that. It is a risk, but it depends on the personality that you are, and where you come from.

Participant 1: It seems like I have to forget that I am unlimited to do that. I wouldn't need this admiration from the crowd.

Joachim: That's wonderful to hear, but there are so many out there who just need it. Everybody who is on stage, every actor, they are addicts. They need the attention of the others, and the moment you are on the needle of attention, you will want it again, and again. And, you want more and more and more of it. The dose needs to get higher.

If you are not attracted to getting attention... very good. If you are, be careful. That's about the only advice I can give. There's nothing wrong with trying to teach other people, but it's a great challenge to stay who you are if others come and tell you how great you are; a big challenge. And then you might start again with the human games even though you were so close.

Participant 1: I'm not saying I'm there totally. I forget, and slip back and my ego comes in, but I'm aware. I think this is the truth; it's been so powerful for me doing the exercises, it's close to a year now. I see the physical changes. Thank you.

Joachim: In my experience it's also beyond what words can explain, for it's so simple. It goes back to the very basics. It's like all needs are satisfied, but the entire human life is about satisfying needs. So, suddenly you are free. It doesn't mean you don't go out and enjoy a walk in nature or enjoy good music, no, but you don't have to do it in order to be satisfied, and this makes a big difference.

Anybody have any other comments?

Participant 2: I have a question, especially about cultivating our awareness. It has to do with how the breath kind of slows down and becomes more subtle. I think it's becoming more and more frequent and also more intense, my reaction to the subtlety of the breath, almost like its lacking, and I start to react more and more to it. Before, I could be more at peace with it, but now as I become more aware of certain things in my body that "lack of breath," let's call it, starts to trigger, and I become more frustrated about it and I kind of have to take a very deep breath in, and it just takes it back... I don't know if you could say something about that?

Joachim: Yes, that's the price we have to pay. That's the fine print. But it's so fine printed, it's hard to read! As you get more sensitive, well, you sense more! Surprise! And many things you sense that you haven't sensed before are not that pleasurable. And I have to say, it doesn't get better! (*laughter*)

The more sensitive you get, the more you will sense. There are so many emotions in your body that are so strongly conditioned, that you say, "Well, I'm just the victim of my emotions." Also, there is such a huge latency between becoming aware of something and the response of the physical body. At some point you realize, "Oh, something has just triggered me. I'm angry." But all the chemicals are already floating in your body. They keep you angry for a while, because it takes some time for them to dissolve. And as long as they are active, you are still angry or upset.

130

But then – here is the point – stay in clarity, don't act it out if possible.

It's true, it's kind of frustrating. At the same time, even that passes, because that also calms down. It becomes the new level of sensitivity, and you can deal with it. You will develop the capacity.

You'll realize more and more, *this is not me, even though I sense it*. It is, in a way, so close, and you believe this still to be your body.

And then, at some point, you'll sense more and more mass consciousness, which is never very pleasant.

Well, you have to get used to that and try not to be torn away or influenced by it too much. But there is no end to that. This is one of the reasons why I would say that many of the enlightened beings leave, for it's just too much. Sensing so much of what you are actually not interested in, getting accustomed to it, and continually letting it go... this is not an easy task.

So, yes, that's the way it is. So, congratulations! You are coming to the fine print.

5. How Core Beliefs Shape the Experienced Reality

Welcome back everybody! We are already at the fifth session of our ten week program, so the first half is nearly over. We'll have an intense session today, and then we'll go into the second part and way beyond the physical body. Today we have the final session concerning the physical vessel, and as usual, we start out with cultivating the awareness. Then we will go into the topic of the day which is "How core beliefs shape the experienced reality." That's the theme for today.

So everybody, please stretch your backbone, sit straight; take on the royal posture. That's most important, the royal posture. Take on the inner feeling of awe for what you are doing. It's most important that you truly know that this is a direct way to enlightenment and not just some causal exercise like stretching your body or your muscles. No, it's going directly to the core of enlightenment.

So, stretch the backbone, pull in the chin a little bit, push the head against the sky. Feel all your body weight pressing on your buttocks. Everything along the vertical line from your crown to your buttocks you can just let go. Let the shoulders fall back a little so the chest opens up and you can breathe deeper.

The eyes are three quarters closed and the gaze is directed downward about forty-five degrees without focusing on anything, which means the energy of vision goes within.

The mouth is closed. The tongue is touching the roof of the mouth and the upper teeth from behind. You are breathing in and out through your nose.

I remind you that this is not about achieving anything, not about perfecting yourself, not about becoming better or "a good breather," or a "good posture-haver." No, it is just coming back to your natural state.

In order to come back to your natural state, you just stop doing what gets you out of your natural state. Like following your thoughts, being in your dreams, being in the tomorrow or the yesterday. Instead, be just here now. Whenever you feel you are torn away by anything, you just come back. You come back to your breath; the breath is always with you. So, become aware of your breath.

Becoming aware of your breath means that you notice how the air enters your nose as a draft. You can feel a coolness in your nose. You can feel your chest move. You can feel your belly move. You can be aware of all of this simultaneously, which implies that you are beyond your mind, for the linear mind wouldn't be able to do that.

Now become aware of the tiny, tiny movements of your spine of your backbone while you are breathing. If your belly moves, then the balance needs to be reestablished; your upper body needs to be balanced through your muscles. There are tiny, tiny movements everywhere, just become aware of that.

Again, stretch your backbone. Become as large as you could possibly be; notice the difference.

Become aware of your left leg, your entire left leg.

First, you notice the existence of the leg. Then you might feel the temperature, the tissue on your skin. With the awareness comes the relaxation. All tension goes away. And a funny thing happens! The relaxation spreads out to the right leg, even though your awareness wasn't actively placed there. Well, presence is infectious; it spreads, it gets "bigger."

Now become consciously aware of your right leg.

It's interesting, when you ask yourself, "What is it that I become aware of? Is it the bones, the cells, the blood, the skin? What is it, precisely? Is it the feeling of touch? All of the above?"

Once again, stretch your backbone and notice its movement. You have sunk back into your "normal" position, and if you stretch it again, you are usually astonished at how big you can get, even though you hadn't noticed how you'd shrunk in.

Now become aware of your left arm, from the shoulders, to your fingertips.

Include your right arm.

Now add to your awareness both of your shoulders and your throat.

Expand your awareness to the muscles of your mouth, and your lips. Feel all the fine muscles on your face. They are connected to the emotional body. They express your inner state of feeling at every given moment. If you relax those muscles, your inner state relaxes also.

Now do the same with your eyes. Become aware of your eye balls, your eye lids, and all the muscles around your eyes.

Now feel the skin of your head, all the skin, not just your face.

Now the top of your head, your crown.

The back of your head.

The skin around your ears. If you can, move your ears. Do it right now, and feel the skin moving, feel all the muscles that are located there.

Now become aware of the skin that is directly located next to your spine on your back. Again, stretch your spine. Feel the skin on your back along your spine.

Now feel all of your skin – from the crown to the feet, from your back to your belly, arms, legs, ears.

Wonderful! Now open up totally. Let go of the concentration on your body, and just be present. One might say, forget about your body and just become aware of whatever your body presents to you as sensations, as stimuli, but do not act on those. Observe, and let go. If a car is driving by and there is a sound, you just let it go. If a muscle is itching or twitching, you just notice and let it go. You do not move, there's no need to move; same with your thoughts. Observe, and let go.

Sometimes you might even notice how you are stuck in the awareness of a muscle. You are following your breath and realize there is some stuck energy; in a way, you might get stuck also in that muscle. The moment you notice that, let it go. Open up and come back to pure awareness without focusing. That way, you release all stress in that muscle. You don't want to change the muscle. You allow it to be as it is right now. It is this allowing, this accepting, that changes everything.

This is the most important part of cultivating your awareness. Becoming aware of your body is just the entry step, but then the deconditioning has to take place, and this is how you do it: you observe, and let go – over and over again. The moment you realize you have gotten stuck in your thoughts or whatever, you stretch the backbone once again and assume the position of clarity. You become aware of your breath, and then you go back into observing mode. That way you are actively stepping out of the dream over and over and over again.

There will be days when this is very easy, when you are very clear, calm, balanced, and open. And on other days, it will be very difficult, but that doesn't matter! You just do the very same. Always come back to the now moment, to the now of your body, stretching the backbone, observing the breath, and start over.

From today on, we will add a new element after cultivating the awareness. Thus, when you cultivate your awareness on your own, don't do what I invite you to do now. You should really separate these things for cultivating the awareness is simple, it's utmost simplicity. This is where you should develop your mastery in.

However, there are some helpers that we can use and that we will use. One of those helpers is becoming aware of your belly right now, the center of your belly, what is called the Hara. It's inside your belly, below your navel. Feel deeply into that location, into that spot. Place your awareness there, and get in resonance with you Hara.

There is, so to speak, a "sound" emanating from that location. You might sense it, hear it internally, or imagine it; it's a deep sound. It's a sound that's not for the ears. It's a joyful sound.

So, if you sense it, get in resonance with it and feel it. If you don't sense it, well, then intone it inwardly. Create that sound by yourself; say, a deep humming sound. But you are absolutely free to find a sound, like humming or a vowel, that fits best for you. It's a continuous sound, it doesn't waver. And it spreads out; it's kind of a carrier.

Imagine that sound spreading out of this location and permeating all of your body. It spreads through all of your body, and even beyond. A deep humming sound.

During the next week, when you are in your daily life, once in a while you might sense into this humming sound within you – whenever you think of it. And notice the changes that will go on in your body as soon as you notice it, as soon as you allow it to spread through your body.

Good, we will now play some music and Althar will join us.

*

I am Althar, the Crystal Dragon.

What a delight it is to be with you once again!

It's only our fifth session, and to me it feels like we have been together much longer, and maybe we have. Maybe we have met long, long ago. And maybe, we had other sessions in other realms, preparing for this.

Now you are here in your physical vessel, trying to embody, in a way, what you have already learned in other sessions. We repeat it here, so it can sink in; sink into your human consciousness, which will then allow you to open up beyond human consciousness.

Today's topic is *core beliefs*, which I sometimes also call *core intents*. I usually use them synonymously, for what starts out as an intent oftentimes becomes a belief – it goes into auto repeat mode. The reason why the original intent came into place may be forgotten, but its effects stay in place as a core belief.

So it doesn't really matter if I use the term core intent or core belief, for the effect is the same. I use the term "core" to emphasize that you cannot easily let go of these beliefs or intents. You might be able to let go of a small intent, a small belief, like the party you usually vote for, but the core beliefs are deeply, deeply engrained in what is called the blueprints and the DNA. So you cannot easily go beyond them. However, it is crucial, very crucial, to have a good understanding of how these core beliefs and core intents determine the experiences of your existence.

As a human, you are mainly bound by three core intents. The first is time. Time forces you into a linear mode. Whatever happens is interpreted by you on a cause and effect basis. This is absolutely crucial to finally go beyond separation, for this allows you to really dissect and investigate in slow motion what happens when you have an intent and how it is reflected. In particular, when your intent is reflected in the physical – when you have a physical mirror – you see in slow motion what an intent does and how it plays out in the playground that you are existing in as a human.

The second core intent is space. Space allows you to have a physical body and lures you into the belief that you actually are a physical body, located at a specific point in space. At this spot, you have your center of perception and experience. From this perspective, you experience your environment.

And then there is a third core intent, which is veiling your origin, veiling your true self. As a human, you do not know where you come from. This is unique amongst all creatures in existence. Every other creature knows about its true self or is at least "semi aware" of the bond to the true self it came from.

Humans don't have that. That's why they are usually in great fear of death. Your animals for instance, well, they are also physical beings, but when their time has come, they are not fighting as much for their life as the humans do. At some point, they just relax; they give in and change their perspective. "Be done with it! Game over, let's have another round!" They do not hang on so much to their lives. But the humans, oh they have veiled their origins, and so there are all kinds of beliefs around death and life after death and myths about who is coming to save you.

So these are the three core intents a human is bound to. As you go into embodied ascension it is not that you have to shed these core intents. It would be very difficult for you to maintain your physical composition, your physical structure, if you tried. So, it's not about destroying them, or totally letting them go. No, it's about understanding them, understanding the purpose they serve, understanding the limitations they create, but then going beyond them; playing with them, but being beyond nevertheless.

This is far, far more difficult than it sounds. It's very easy to wrap your head around the mechanics of core intents and core beliefs. You know you needed some common rules on the playground, otherwise you couldn't share experiences with each other. That's not that difficult to understand.

However, it *is* difficult to understand, to grasp or sense *beyond* your core beliefs – specifically if those core beliefs are time and space.

So, today we are tempting to do just that. We attempt to give you an idea of what it means to be

141

bound by core beliefs in a different way then you are used to.

We will do this using some geometrical examples. *Geometry!* Geometry can be very interesting, and very sensual if you allow it to be. The big advantage that we have with using geometry is that you do not have emotional attachments to, say, dots, line segments, circles, or anything like that. It's kind of neutral for you, I guess. Thus, you can go in there and experience it without all kinds of memories coming up and bothering you. Thus, I invite you today to get very experiential with geometry.

To do so, please start by going back to when you were, say, eight years old. Eight is a good age. You are not a small child anymore, and you are not yet in puberty, no hormones are bothering you. You are kind of open to existence and don't get too mental. So, become eight years old again.

Imagine a Sunday afternoon. It's raining outside, you have nothing do. It's kind of boring, but you feel fine. And then suddenly, you hear this, say, crystal clear voice from within. It's telling you, "Sit at your desk. Take out a blank sheet of paper and a pencil." Feel into this scenario. Be in your room that you had as a child, sit at your desk. Look through the eyes of that child. See the sheet of paper and the pencil that you've placed before you. Now that voice tells you to draw a straight line all over the page, from one edge to the other, one straight line. So you do; one straight black line on a white sheet of paper. Then the voice continues, "Imagine that line spreads out into infinity, on both sides of the page, far, far beyond the page."

The image appears immediately in your mind and it's kind of interesting just to see that. The crystal clear voice continues with saying, "Focus on that line. Feel that line. Sense that line." Then it adds, "Why don't you dive into that line and experience how life within a line is?"

So you stare and focus at the line. You realize that this line is actually made of dots! There are many, many dots making up this line. So you fall into the line, and become a dot! Suddenly, forgetting all of your human existence, you are just a dot. Well, you cannot do much, but it is exciting. All of your senses are gone. You are living in, well, a kind of line that you cannot even see. But what you can do is move to the left and the right, even though you don't know what left and right is. But there are, let's say, two directions you can move in. That is what you can do.

So you try to move. You are moving along that line and you pass through many other dots, which is kind of interesting, but also weird! But who cares, you can do that as a dot!

It's really exciting! You can move slowly, you can move fast. You can move with the speed of light. Life as a dot – that is interesting and so very different from that of you as a human child; suddenly you have such different capabilities.

So, you continue to exist as a dot in your line and, in a way, the time passes. You get accustomed to the circumstances, you feel fine as a dot.

One morning, when you walk along the line, so to speak, you encounter another dot. And the dot says, "I am a scientist. I am a scientist, and I discovered something great! I discovered the notion of *distance*. Distance allows you to *measure* how far two dots are away from each other." He then tells you all the tricks and gives you a ruler, so you can also measure!

Well, it's a bit difficult for a dot to carry a ruler, but somehow this works out! And you realize, wow, on this ruler, there are centimeters on it! Isn't that great? So these dots are also smart. They have never heard of a foot, or a yard, or an inch, or anything like that. They don't come up with confusing base units for measuring distance, no. They start out with meters and centimeters right away.

So you have your ruler at hand and you apply it. And life is suddenly different. You get a new understanding of life on the line. Everything is different now. You can measure the distances between any two dots. You know how far you have traveled this day and yesterday. Wonderful! It's even like a kind of creation, a creation in the realm of dots and of straight lines.

One day, you might say it was raining again, a rainy Sunday afternoon in your line, and you didn't really know what to do as a dot. So you went into daydreaming mode and pondered,

"Well, I am a dot… But who am I really? *Who am I really?*" Well obviously, as a dot living on the line, you think that you probably are a tiny, tiny line yourself – a line segment. A dot must be a piece of a line! Otherwise, how could there be a line in the first place?

But then you ask yourself, "Well, I assume I am a small, small line segment, that appears to be a dot, but how large am I?" So you take your ruler and start measuring. "How large am I? Maybe one centimeter?" So you check the ruler and notice, "One centimeter away from me there is another dot called Paul, I know him." Well, Paul is obviously not you, so you know you must be smaller than one centimeter.

Okay, so you try with a millimeter. Again, there is another dot. You know him also. And that's not you, so you must be smaller. So you continue with a micrometer, a nanometer, and so forth. At some point you realize, "No matter how small I make myself, there is always, always another dot at what should be my boundary!" And you suddenly feel those dots are very intrusive. They are so close! You never noticed this before, but now that you can measure, wow, they are so close, and you don't like that too much.

So you try even smaller and smaller distances until you suddenly realize, "Wait a minute! I can go as small as I like, but unless I go to zero distance, there will always be another dot within what I want to be me. But if I go to zero, then I will go out of existence! I will cease to be a dot!

There will be no 'dot-ness' left within me. I will be wiped out. I would wipe myself out if I continue this line of thought!" That was scary, really scary.

Oh, the dots, they have heard stories about two god beings. There was *the pencil!* A pencil that could create dots out of nothing! And another story was about *the rubber*. The rubber could erase a whole line, and all dots would just be extinguished.

But these stories were just hearsay, they seemed to be far-fetched. No one had ever seen the pencil or the rubber. Whether they exist or not, you don't know, but what you *do* know is that when you apply distance to yourself, you go out of existence. And that is scary! So you stop thinking along that line. You want to be at least a tiny line segment! *Even if it is just a belief, you don't care!* You are now used to the life of a dot. You have so many dot companions. You know what they do; they know you, you know them, you are friends or not. But at least you know that you exist as a dot. And so you throw away your ruler and decide you never, ever, ever want to measure yourself again.

At that very moment, you as the eight year old daydreaming child wake up and think, "Oh, that was intense! That was the life of a dot, or the life of a non-existing line segment, a one dimensional creature – a one dimensional creature, very interesting. But what would happen if I went into two dimensions? Two dimensions instead of one."

Suddenly, you hear that crystal clear voice from within saying, "Take a new sheet of paper!" And so you do. You leave it blank and go directly into your imagination. You ask yourself, "Well, if there was a dot somewhere on that page and I applied the notion of distance, what would happen?"

Well, on a line, distance would create a line segment of a certain length. But what about a plane? On your sheet of paper, this would create a circle! All the dots that are within a certain radius form a circle! So, if you existed on a plane, you would become a circle!

And so you do! You jump right into that sheet of paper and take on the vessel of a circle. Compared to your life as a dot, this is very different. Incomparable! Suddenly, you can move in two dimensions. And that's an infinite number of directions, not just two, as in a line. You can float along on the sheet of paper and beyond. That's very, very different from the life as a dot. But then, the very same thing as before happens again. At some point, you want to measure how big you are. Well, you take the ruler – which you know from your previous incarnation, somehow the knowledge came with you – and you apply the ruler to yourself. Once again, you realize, as a circle, you are just a bag of dots! Just a bag of dots; so many dots that aren't you! So how large is the circle that you believe yourself to be *really*? Well, you cannot measure it. You again have to go to zero distance to not find any dot that you do not want to be.

And again the fear arises in you. "Wow, I believed myself to be a circle and it felt really good, but I cannot put my finger on what that circle really is; I cannot put my finger on myself. I would again go out of existence if I continued measuring myself."

You, as an eight year old child, meanwhile got used to this insight, and say, "Yeah, okay, I started with a dot and the notion of distance in one dimension, and became a line segment. Then I added another dimension and became a circle. But what does a line segment have to do with a circle? They are so different. Therefore, let's go into three dimensions, for that must be really interesting."

If you take a dot and some distance in three dimensions, then you get a sphere, a ball of a certain radius. All the dots around some origin that you pick arbitrarily, well, they form a sphere, an interesting 3D object! But as you exist already in 3D with your physical body, you do not even have to imagine it. But a sphere has the very same problem as a circle and a line segment: it's just a bag of dots, and you cannot put your finger on the beingness of a sphere, other than recognizing that it stems from a belief. A belief made up somewhere – somewhere in consciousness.

Now, you, as an eight year old child, you have a look at your physical body and ask yourself, "Well, what *am* I? How *big* am I? Obviously, I am not a sphere – well, if I eat enough, I become like a sphere, so I am a kind of sphere – but I am full of matter, not dots." However, you have heard in a documentary on TV that nobody really knows what matter is. Moreover, what they actually do know is that matter does not consist of matter. So, in a way, you are not that different from a line segment, or circle, or sphere. *You are not! You don't know what you are,* and as soon as you start measuring yourself, you get into problems.

The funny thing is, as you realize now as a grown-up, or as your eight year old, that you need the notion of distance – which is just a synonym for separation – to even come into existence. Only with the notion of distance do you come into existence. There is a circle only with the notion of separation, of distance. But, if you apply distance to yourself – well, *you vanish!* Isn't that crazy? What kind of crazy belief is "separation" in the first place? That's very, very weird!

Let that sink in for a moment. Feel into this. Feel how life changed from living on a line to living as a circle to living as a sphere.

*

Obviously, I used dimensions to represent core beliefs. In this specific example, each core belief is essentially the same: it's a spatial dimension. But, isn't it interesting what these imply? When you start out with one spatial dimension and use the concept of distance then you end up with a line segment. You add another spatial dimension and you have a totally different experience as a circle. Then you add a third spatial dimension and get a sphere; again, a totally different geometrical entity. Now imagine that these objects were actually living beings, then they could not really relate to each other. How could a dot relate to a sphere? How could a sphere relate to a circle? Well, a sphere could maybe "somehow" relate to a circle, because it's a special case of a sphere – you can shrink or compress a sphere and you come close to a circle – but how a real circle feels in its 2D shape, a sphere will never know.

The same holds for humans. You can never know for sure how the existence in another realm, which is based on other core beliefs, feels like. You can talk about it, but actually you have no way to project another realm into your 3D consciousness. It's more or less impossible!

Just try it! We've gone from 1D to 2D to 3D by just adding spatial dimensions. Now, let's go 4D. What would a sphere look like in 4D?

Your imagination just fails, right? There is no way, no way for a human to relate to a 4D sphere. Well, you can do mathematical calculations with it, it's just the same as with a 3D or 10D sphere, but if you want to picture it, well, it's not possible. You fail! You fail, because your consciousness is so limited that you simply cannot picture it.

Now take a realm with multiple dimensions that are not spatial, like having two timelines in parallel. You can say, well, humans have half of a dimension called time which only goes in one direction, it never goes backwards, but what would your experience be if you had two time-lines, or three or four timelines? Combined with six spatial dimensions... your imagination gives up. *You have no way of imaging that!* And *that* you have to understand. That's why I brought you into the geometrical arena: to really make you understand what you don't know.

However, there are two things you should remember. There is something that all these geometrical entities have in common. And they share this with all entities in all of creation: they share the fear of being extinguished – because the vessel that they believe themselves to be is not real in the first place. And every entity, no matter where it exists, knows that somewhere deep down inside.

If an entity scratches the surface of itself, it will find emptiness, and that is scary. That is why there is this big, big fear of being wiped out throughout all of existence. And actually, this is why you are here as humans. Oh, the human often thinks, "Let's go up the dimensional ladder! Add some more dimensions, more core beliefs, or less core beliefs – however you want to phrase it – and have a broader experience."

Yes, you can do that, and actually you did that already! *You came from there*, from all those realms. You have been there. But no matter where you have been, you found out that the vessel that you believed yourself to be, be it in form, or beyond form, did not really exist! But you were not able to accept that and to let go of separation.

That's why you finally ended up here, as a human, on planet Earth in a slow motion physical reality with your three core beliefs: time, space, and the veiling of your origin.

The point I want to make is: *do not try to go back to the higher dimensional existences! It doesn't bring you anywhere!* You came from there. You are here to come out, in a way, at the other end of the tunnel. You are in the lowest density, in the deepest density. Here you can go *beyond* the belief of separation. You can go beyond all the vessels, you see?

You can go beyond all the vessels that you ever believed yourself to be, and you can do it on behalf of your true self and all the emanations your true self ever had!

Compared to angelic beings, you may feel like a dot; very limited. But I tell you what: *you are the hero in existence!* You are the hero in all of existence.

It's not about going back. It's about going beyond!

Now, to add to this geometrical experience, let's have some music, and we'll have a little journey. Again, I want you to become very, very playful and imaginative. For we are going to visit, and to sense, into other emanations of your true self – and as we have seen with the geometrical example, it is very difficult to picture those. Don't even try, just sense into them, and the music is there to stimulate you.

(Music plays)

In the course of last week, a call went out from your true self to inform representatives of all of its emanations to be very present today. So, you might say, they are very close. Right now, they radiate out. Oh, you cannot see them, and if you could, you would see what a line would see of a circle, not too much. But that's not the reason why we are doing this.

First, feel into the entities that are coming close right now. They make themselves "feelable." It's very difficult to describe these entities, for I need to use human terminology, and well, that just doesn't really work. But to get an idea of them, imagine: what does it mean to live as a fog, as a cloud, as a fragrance?

How does it feel to live as part of a swarm, to not be an individual at all? Have you ever thought about that? You are one in the many – unconnected even – but still somehow kind of a vessel, a swarm body.

How does a body feel that responds immediately to your every intent? Without delay, without any latency?

How fast would such a body move, or change its form?

Imagine two of those beings fighting with each other, just because they can.

If you don't have a physical body, then nothing that you do has severe consequences for you. You

153

feel no pain, no physical pain as humans know it. So, nothing is that serious, other than for the ego, which is of course always serious, no matter your form. Without physical pain, you don't need to be so cautious.

There are realms without humor. Can you imagine that? Entities that have never heard a joke, or laughed at each other or about themselves – never ever, no humor!

There are realms without empathy, without compassion. There's just greed, just survival, only *more*; more, more, more – just hierarchy, climbing the ladder, eat or be eaten.

There are so many different ways to experience all of this, but in the end, well, it's always the same. It's the mantra of *enough is not enough*; give me *more* experiences. Give me more, or less, core beliefs to experience in playgrounds. Let me try this, let me try that. And after a while, after a while of being a dot or a line or a circle or a sphere, you always come to the conclusion, "*I am not real*, even though I may distract myself for a long time in this new playground. But then I always come to the very same conclusion. Who am I? *I have no clue!* But if I go into this line of thinking any further, I might be extinguished."

So many different entities!

Now consider planet Earth, floating in space.

Consider the humans and the human DNA.

Whatever you can experience "out there" in

any of those playgrounds defined by the core beliefs, there is a version or variant of it brought to this planet; brought right into your DNA, so that you can act it out, so that you can experience it – in a specific form of course, adapted to your special playground. But it relates on a one to one basis to the other realms.

That's why you have so many different characters amongst humans. You can live totally without empathy, or love. You can live totally just in the physical, or in the arts, or in science. You have all options here and you can change as much as you like in a given lifetime. *Nothing really holds you back from doing that other than yourself.*

As humans, you experience all of this in slow motion! And at some point in your many, many lifetimes you came to the conclusion: *enough!* Just enough! Enough repetitions! Even though the mantra of separation is "Enough is never enough," you said "Enough!" And in doing so, you broke the cycle. Then you started your search, your spiritual search.

You searched, and you searched, and you searched, and you searched... until once again you said, "Enough! Enough searching! I'm done with it! I'm done with the outer search, and I'm done with the inner search!" Then it didn't take you long to end up here, in this very now moment.

Meanwhile, you had your moments of enlightenment; you had your moments beyond separation. You had your moments of "I know that I know." Moments of "I am that I am."

This is the true wisdom that liberates, that doesn't need any measurement system, or any separation. It stands on its own. And now, as we are here in this sacred moment, radiate that out to all your cousins that your true self has emanated. To do so, why not just go right into your true self? Imagine your true self to be a sun; go into that sun! Don't hesitate, you have nothing to lose. You cannot burn; it's not too hot, just go in there; it's the best feeling ever.

This sun has so many rays. Imagine those rays to be the emanations of your true self. Oh, they've reached out far, reached out into so many playgrounds, experienced and experienced, searched and searched, just as you did. Beyond time, in time; beyond space, in space; in realms you could not imagine as a human.

The one thing that all of these emanations share with you is that you all came from the same true self and in the end, you were all searching for the same true wisdom. And you have found it! Now radiate it out! Radiate that out into all the rays of your true self.

I am that I am – without definition.

I know that I know.

Let that radiate out, and they will pick it up in their own way. They will pick it up when the time is right. It arrives as a potential, a strong, strong potential, and suddenly they might hear a voice, a crystal clear voice from within, telling them to do something, and they just follow it. Somehow, it will work out.

Can a sphere relate to a point? Well, maybe it can imagine being a point, but can it feel the life of a point? No, not really.

Maybe that is the reason why, let's say, God consciousness cannot feel into separation at all. You have to be in separation to be able to experience it. So in a way, God cannot help you. He doesn't really know about you.

In this very moment, you are beyond separation, you are God also! You do not need any help!

That is a discovery you can make only on Earth as a human. Going into the deepest density, becoming a dot so to speak, and then dropping out of the dimensions – going beyond – not binding yourself by a stupid measurement system, be it a ruler, or the belief in separation in general.

Now, become aware of your human consciousness. Let go of the notion of time. It's not about your current lifetime. It's about the now and the totality of all that you are.

Let go of the notion of space, go beyond it. You are not here anyway.

Let go of the notion of separation.

And you are instantly, instantly, instantly in your natural state.

Because you have been here, because you have experienced time, space, and the veiling of your origin, because you have also been in all of the other realms – oh, you can now be truly an ambassador of creation, of true creation.

Letting go of the core beliefs doesn't prohibit you from using them to your advantage. Thus, you can let go of space and time, yet still *be* in the physical, but you are not bound by it anymore.

What a journey. What a journey!

*

Even though it doesn't seem to fit, I remind you of the daily homework: cultivate your awareness. Do not miss that chance. The experiences we just had are wonderful, but bring them even more to life, day in, day out. And to be able to do so, you have to become the master of your physical vessel. It's not a fight; it's a coming back to the natural state. It's a deconditioning. And nobody can do it but you.

Also, throughout the day, whenever it occurs to you, become aware of that deep, deep sound within you; how it caresses you, how it spreads out through your body and even beyond. Note what happens if you become aware of that sound.

I am Althar the Crystal Dragon. Once again it was great to witness all the beauty that comes forth when consciousness opens up, and I look forward to seeing you soon again, next week – until then. Good bye.

*

Joachim: So, time for remarks, questions, or silence.

Participant 1: Well, first of all, it was an amazing session today, especially going to the core beliefs and seeing them so clearly. And what I'm experiencing actually since we started the whole Althar series is that when I am doing the Light Body Exercise, I have a really hard time to go into the safety part of it. I have no problem with love, have no problem with the clarity, it's the safety, and sometimes I just cannot get over that hurdle. And, probably related to that, in my human experience I get now all these worries about not having a house, all those kinds of things that are, you know, that normally I wouldn't really be worried about. It's kind of like everything comes together in that fear of extinction that you were mentioning today.

Joachim: And the lack of safety is actually that which you really can't compensate for as long as you believe yourself to be a physical body.

And while many might claim they have overcome this... Yeah, sure, it's not that easy. I always have this example: if you think you have overcome it, stop breathing and count until 1000! Truly! It doesn't take too long and the body takes over, no matter what you say, because the body itself has a kind of fear. It wants to survive, and this makes becoming aware of the feeling of safety difficult.

So, you cannot force becoming aware of safety. Therefore, I say it's easiest to start from relative safety. Thus, you recall a situation that wasn't safe at all, like being in the midst of an earthquake, or whatever might have happened in your life that was truly unsafe, and you were absolutely helpless and couldn't do anything about it. As opposed to now, where it's relatively safe – relatively – a meteor could come at any minute, but usually they don't, so right now you are kind of safe. Then feel the difference and go from there. Do not think that this is not good enough. Safety is actually really difficult. But when it comes, even in small doses... Don't think of absolute safety, but when it comes in small doses, oh there's already a wonderful relaxation in the body. Just continue doing that. It's not a rush, so observe what goes on as you slowly get used to the feeling of safety. Go slowly, and just continue doing it.

Participant 1: Thank you.

Joachim: I always try to look someone in the eye, but I find it difficult doing this via Zoom! I can look at the grid, but no one feels I am peering at him. Now I am peering at Z***. Who the hell is Z***? Oh the speechless boy! (*chuckles*). He cannot talk. Ahh he can! (*Z*** unmutes himself.*) There he is!

Participant 2: I had many, many questions five days ago. I wanted to write them down and everything. And suddenly they were all so compound and direct in my head. I was very happy to ask all these questions in the moment you were telling this story, this for me very funny story, being an eight year old boy, or girl. In my case boy!

Joachim: Good you say it – you don't know these days!

Participant 2: It was really just wonderful! In a way, I am still inside.

Joachim: In general, if there are questions, it's always good to write them down, because the process of writing them down lets them go out of your head. Then the answer might come to you directly, or you might send an email to me and I might try to answer it. Maybe it helps, maybe not, but at least the question is formulated, it's crystallized, so the thinking clears up a little bit and you might get a new perspective on the real problem beneath that. And if it's answered that way, that's the best, right?

Participant 2: Meanwhile, there are so many questions, and I feel that just asking them would be – in a certain way it's overwhelming. Writing them down for me and not sending them to you in a certain way is also like a relief, because like you said, or what I understood – I give the answer to myself, or the answer is already in me.

Joachim: Give me an example.

Participant 2: Well, the moment you say, "The dragon says," so to speak, or to "be inside the emotional body" to dissolve it – I try to practice that and I totally get it, but sometimes, maybe it's because I'm an actor, something comes in and says that's ridiculous – it feels like "Oh my God, I'm a dragon now!" I don't know how to say it in English…

Joachim: It's "making fun of it."

Participant 2: Yes, making fun of it. I love humor so much. It's such a distraction for me also. And like anyway, emotions. I was a drama guy, I still am, and a lot of parts of me are. I don't want to say that this is a problem, but I need lots of awareness and a lot of dragon breath to dissolve these emotional body issues.

Joachim: Let me clarify one point. The dissolving is passive. When you say, "I go into the emotional body in order to dissolve it," well, that is kind of right, but the better notion is, you become aware of it and as you do, it just dissolves. It's not that you go in with a sword, and cut it to pieces! No, you become aware of what is going on and by not fueling all those feedback loops continually, well, they will just fall apart. And it's passive, that is the one thing that's so important

Everything here is passive!

You don't go out, mostly, and push anything. *Nothing stands pure consciousness*! That is maybe the best mantra as opposed to *enough is not enough*. Nothing stands pure consciousness! The moment you are in your clarity, the body can do its dance as it likes, but you don't give a shit, plainly said!

If you feel like a dragon, well, there's much to it. That was the reason, why I didn't kick Althar out of the books, because I had the same feeling. When I had the first dragon experience, of course I searched the internet, what else, and I came across the strangest communities. People believing they are dragons, but disguised as humans, and they make their nests and eggs, and hoo-oo, that's creepy, huh? But hey, who knows what's going on in the world, I don't know.

For me, the dragon experience was strange. The general thing is: you are what you believe yourself to be. Now, what beliefs do you choose? Sure, you have the core beliefs, and those core beliefs are so strong that you cannot easily let them go, no matter what you tell yourself. But beyond that, you are really what you believe yourself to be. That's how you become a good actor. You believe yourself to be so and so on stage, then so you are. Bad luck if you cannot get out of that role afterwards, but everybody is an actor in that respect.

So, you can act as a dragon, you can even perceive yourself as a dragon. But others will usually not do so. And that's actually the difference between core beliefs and private beliefs. Core beliefs are typically shared. That's why we have a shared environment, a shared experience. Whatever goes on in your strange mind, or mine, is, I wouldn't say totally private, but it's not so easily shared with others. We can have an opinion about, I don't know, the Zoom interface that we see, but still everybody sees a different thing. So, you might perceive yourself as a dragon, and others might also sense you as a dragon, but they will certainly not see the form of a dragon that you see.

So, that's the personal beliefs versus core beliefs. Understanding that you are in essence whatever you choose to be, well, that's liberating, and of course frightening, when your emotional body comes in between and cries out, "Hey, what about me? I'm also still here, take care of me."

Good. Another question?

Participant 3: In that sense, I sometimes wonder, is it ever possible to really, really go beyond all those, you know, beyond separation and be in a body at the same time.

Joachim: Yeah, your have to find out for yourself. That's an honest answer! But the best answer I'm aware of is: it's always possible in the moment! In the moment! And that is the greatest relief! You can be enlightened in the moment, but continually being enlightened is difficult. So, hey, start with the moment! What comes out of a moment of enlightenment is usually good! How long that moment will last you don't know, because this moment is beyond time anyway.

So, if you are sitting here as a dot and all the beliefs are piling up on you, and it looks ugly, like there's no way to get out, because it all presses down on you. Somehow, all the dimensions are weighing on you. However, the moment you get beyond that, you are just out. Like this, without any process!

That's the crazy thing; it's a shift in perspective! Now, you cannot hold that for too long, because you are so used to all of it; you are so used to believing you are still a body, you are still connected to your body.

The dot says, "I'm not living along this line anymore." And the line says, "Where did you go, dot? Come back to me, otherwise I'll come after you!" And the line will! Just like the cells will cry out to your consciousness, the body will continue breathing, no matter what you tell it.

But anyway, when I say, "At some point, you shift your center of awareness from the physical body to the light body," you still let the physical body continue to exist as it does! You want that! You want to be able to go into the physical and experience life, share life, and share your experiences.

But at the same time, there is a loosening between the still physically oriented consciousness and the "opened up consciousness." *When* that happens depends on you personally. *If* that happens and *for how long*, who can say? I assume most of you who are here have experienced moments of enlightenment. Well then you can testify: for moments it does work!

And that's the best you can get. We are not getting any guarantee. Just go with that. There is no magic bullet or anything, it is just a letting go, and when a moment of enlightenment happens, you have proof, and then you revert back to limited consciousness.

All of you have been on this road for a long time. If you look back five years, ten years, you notice a difference. There is a noticeable difference. There is an opening up happening. But humans always – oh, I talk of humans as if I'm not a human, but the same holds for me – want it to be so fast. Yeah, but consider this in cosmic dimensions. How long does a sun live – a few billion years?

Now, you are here in your dotty body, supposedly consisting of matter, which you still believe yourself to be, and you have some insights, and some moments of enlightenment, and suddenly all beliefs fall apart? Yeah, it would be nice if that happened, but if it worked out that way, then you would be out. However, you want to stay! Well, then you have to have this ping-pong, this yo-yo effect, going in and out, in and out, until you are suddenly on both sides simultaneously! Or maybe you have to go so fast that you don't notice the difference any more. (*chuckles*)

The trick is not to judge yourself, and to continue. And if it is getting too difficult, check out, so what.

Okay, let's close the session. I'm happy to see you soon, in seven days! Until then, ciao.

6. Your Four Temples

Joachim: Welcome everybody! I see I lost my background, this doesn't work. I just have to figure out where my background has gone. Give me a second.

Participant 1: Being in timeless mode, take all the time you like!

Joachim: Isn't that ugly? A greenscreen with nothing on it? Well, I don't know. We'll leave it as it is, and pretend there is a nice image of something. We will have our eyes closed anyway... but... I don't understand why that is.

Anyway, welcome once again! As usual, we will have our three segments and we will start right away with cultivating the awareness. Take on a royal posture, as always. Stretch your backbone; push your head towards the sky. By doing so, the chin is automatically going in a little bit; the shoulders can fall a little bit backwards, and relax. By stretching the backbone, you can breathe deeply, because then the belly has room to move.

If you have a tight belt, open that belt right now, so you can have your belly move in and out.

Today I want you to have your hand in a specific position. So, I don't know if you can see that. *(Joachim shows his hands to the camera.)*

Place your hands so the middle fingers overlap each other precisely, like this. Then bring your fingers together and have the thumbs meet each other horizontally, like this, like those wonderful Buddha statues, okay?

And then you take this construct and place it so that the little fingers touch your belly. Then the thumbs are right at the height of your Hara.

Okay, now close your eyes three quarters. The tongue is touching the roof of your mouth and the back part of the upper teeth. You breathe in and out through your nose

Just relax. Be aware of the breath coming in and out.

The belly is moving slowly.

Make sure your head is not falling forward, but is upright. If the head is falling forward, first you have a lot of muscle to apply so that it's not falling all the way down to the floor; and also it invites thinking. But right now, it's not about thinking, it's about just being in the now moment. It's difficult to do both. You cannot think and be here-now at the same time. It's just not possible.

This body posture is designed to help you be in the now moment. It's a posture of clarity, of not being distracted by anything – not by thoughts, and not by anything outside of you.

Now become aware of the tips of your thumbs as they are lightly touching each other. The thumbs are horizontal. They do not press against each other and form a kind of a mountain, and they do not fall into your hands. They are resting horizontally, touching each other very lightly.

So, be totally aware of the tips of your thumbs and how they touch each other. This is a very good spot to place your awareness, because you are very sensitive in your fingers, and also it's, let's say, away from your head. If you place your awareness on the lower parts of your body, on your belly or somewhere down there, the mind calms down immediately.

Good. Now expand your awareness to include both of your legs, in their totality, from your feet right up to your buttocks.

(long pause)

Take note of your thumbs once again. Are they still in the position that you brought them into? Are they horizontal? Did you start pressing them against each other? Did they lose contact? If so, just bring them back into the position I described. They are touching each other lightly, and they are horizontal.

Whenever there is stress or tension in your body, it also plays out in your hands, and you can feel it in your thumbs. They start pressing against each other when you think or when you follow some anxious thoughts. And as always, if you then relax your thumbs by means of becoming aware of them, the mind follows and relaxes also.

Now include your belly in your awareness.

Once again, stretch the backbone. Press your head against the sky or the ceiling.

Now include your arms and your chest in your awareness. As you do, remain aware of your thumbs. Do they touch each other?

Include your shoulders and your throat in your awareness.

Now your tongue; the tongue is relaxed, yet lightly touching the teeth and the roof of your mouth.

Now include all of your face in your awareness; your mouth, lips, nose, eyes, cheeks, forehead.

Remain aware of your thumbs and how they are touching each other, and also be aware of the touch of your tongue at the roof of your mouth.

The position of your hands, the way your hands are placed now, is called *the cosmic mudra*. It is as if you held all of existence in your hands. Just imagine that for a moment. And if all of existence is too big, imagine the whole planet Earth in your hands. There's so much going on on planet Earth right now, and you hold it all in your hands.

Okay, now let go of all the body awareness and go beyond. Go just into observing mode; be present – totally present. Whatever comes as a stimulus, as a sensation, take note and let it go.

Whenever you note that you have been distracted, come back to your posture, stretch the backbone, pull in the chin a little bit, push the head against the sky. Check your thumbs; they touch each other lightly. Then let go of this body awareness and go back to observation.

This is the deconditioning! It's maybe the most important step on the road to enlightenment. Without the deconditioning, without the ability to withstand all the sensations and stimuli, it would be very hard to progress.

This is not a fight. It's just being observant, being aware of what's going on, and realizing that there is no need to act on anything!

The body posture helps you in this. Being in a group like this helps you get used to it. Usually, in a group environment, you do not just get up and run out, but you continue. You may have no interest in it. Still, you just continue doing it. And as you get used to it in such a protected environment, it becomes easier and easier to do it also in normal life situations. You can just observe, observe an interaction, without being triggered by any words or the emotional bodies of others.

Once again, become aware of your belly, specifically of your Hara, which is located at the center of your belly, two or three finger widths below the navel. Just like last week, become aware of – or imagine – a deep sound emanating from there.

Now become aware of your chest, the heart area, and listen or imagine a tone that is emanating from there. This tone is usually higher than the one in your belly. They are both in harmony, they fit together.

So, hear those two tones simultaneously; it's like a duet, a choir with two voices.

Now become aware of your crown, the top of your head.

You also can sense a tone there. It's a high pitched tone, usually far beyond what a human can hear. Become aware of that sound, or imagine it, but hold the other two sounds along with it. So we have a chord, a triad.

Sense those three tones simultaneously and feel how they expand. They extend throughout your body and outwards, beyond your body.

Good. Now I will play some music, and then we will see where we go from here.

*

(*Music plays:* "Yesterday was hard on all of us",
Fink)

Lyrics of the song:

Where do we go from here, where do we go?
And is it real or just something we think we
know?
Where are we going now, where do we go?
'Cause if it's the same as yesterday, you know I'm
out
Just so you know

Because, because our paths they cross
Yesterday was hard on all of us
On all of us

And who can we trust from here, who can we
trust?
And are you real or just something from wander-
lust?
Who can you trust from here, sweet flower, who
can you trust?
From cradle to grave, from ashes to ashes
From dust to dust

Because, because our paths they cross
Yesterday was hard on all of us
On all of us

Where do we go from here, where do we go?
And we got nothing we can trust and nothing we
can sell
And how do we get out?

How do we move around with all these eyes on
us?
Tell you what, you go first
It's almost like it's kind of rehearsed

Because, because our paths they cross
Yesterday was hard on all of us
On all of us

*

I am Althar the Crystal Dragon, and I greet you
for this second half of our ten week program.

We have come far in these first five sessions,
and now the question is: *where do we go from
here?* Isn't it interesting that sometimes you come
across a song or lyrics that seem to be made for
you, for your given circumstances? Just like the
song we just heard. This song is called "Yesterday
was hard on all of us." That's true! But "yesterday" is a notion of time. And we have undisguised
time as being merely a symptom of separation. So
yesterday is, in a way, *so* yesterday! Right now,
we are beyond time! You can go beyond time anytime. Anytime you choose! We did that often in
the last five weeks.

Now, where do we go from here? We go into
the surreal. *Into the surreal!* We will go way beyond what the human experiences in his physical
body and in his physical reality. We will go into
the non-physical, and we will walk along the
edges of the world of separation – that is where
we go!

174

The singer asks in the song, "Who can we trust from here?" Who can we, or who can *you* trust from here?

But I tell you what! Trust is also *so* yesterday. Because the moment you had your first moment of enlightenment, trust went out of the window. You do not need trust anymore. Why? Because what is the worst that could happen to you? Nothing! You already *know* that if you let go of everything, you realize that you are All-That-Is. So why would you need trust? You're not like a blind person walking around, not knowing where to go. *No, you have experienced a moment of enlightenment.* And you know what you have to do to become aware of such a moment again.

How? You just *stop* believing. You *sense* into yourself and *you know that you know!* That's it! There is no trust required! It is just a choice that you have to make. As long as you are bound to your physical body, well, you have to make this choice over and over and over again. But that's all! It's about you *remembering* that choice and then making that choice, but you don't need trust. Trust is just not needed anymore.

And then in the song it's said, "I tell you what, *you* go first, it's almost like it's kind of rehearsed." You go first? *Who* goes first? Well, it's up to you, but one thing is sure: it was rehearsed. It was rehearsed in the other realms amongst your spiritual families and amongst those holding the dream of embodied ascension.

However, you can rehearse as often as you like, but at some point you have to make it real by doing it, by allowing to let go of everything, and to open up. That's up to you. You cannot rehearse this; you have to *do* it at some point. And that's why we are here, I guess. Who goes first? Well, actually everybody has to make this step on their own, obviously. But it's so much easier to be in a group like this and also with others from around the planet who aren't here right now and who you know are on the same path as you. So it's not that scary – maybe. But we've heard already, you do not need trust. It's up to you to choose it, and to allow it, to realize it, in every moment.

I always speak of moments of enlightenment, and just like we have moments of enlightenment, we have moments of embodied ascension. That's the way it is. That's the way to go, and, well, who knows, maybe today you will experience just another moment of embodied ascension.

As we go into the surreal, there are a lot of helpers that can be important for you. Therefore, I will talk today about the four temples of you. Your four temples.

The first two temples are in the physical and the other two are in the non-physical.

The first temple is your physical body. You have to make it a temple. See your physical body as a temple and not as a burden! You might say the human body is the pinnacle of creation within separation. It consists of so many building blocks that all interlock. It's a super complex machine that enables you to have the experience of being incarnated.

Even though the body has its ailments, illnesses, problems, and what you might perceive as limitations, it is, well, your temple in which you go towards embodied ascension. It is by means of the body that you do realize enlightenment and embodied ascension.

So how do you make your body into a temple? Well, just by radiating awe towards your body. The body is not your enemy! It's your support. It's your way out of separation. So right now, send a big thank you through your body. Be aware of the feeling of gratitude, of grace. It doesn't matter what happened up to this point with your body, it is because of this body that you are here and that you are seeking to go beyond separation.

This is something that angelic beings always failed at. But you, with your physical body, you can do it! So, there is no need to try to get rid of the physical body or to reject it, or somehow diminish it, no. You become an integrated being! The light body and the physical body will meld, so the physical body will be an integral part of it. It will be the extension of the light body that allows you to act, perceive, and share in the physical.

So, see your physical body as a temple. This is where you live, this is where you practice. Treat your temple well.

The second temple is a physical temple which is usually just a room that belongs to you. It's a room, where you can shut the door and be on your own without being disturbed. Just a simple room to which you say, "This is my temple in the physical." It could be anywhere. It could also be a hut somewhere in the woods. However, it is most important that you have access to it. Why? Because as you go this route into opening up more and more, you need time for yourself. You need time to integrate. You need time without disturbances from the outside, be it family, be it your job, or be it your neighbors. You want to be on your own once in a while to integrate.

And there is not much needed for this kind of physical temple. It's not that you have to build a pyramid or cathedral. It is again the feeling that you have towards this location. If you feel a kind of awe or sacredness in some spots like churches or ancient temples, then this is usually because of the feelings that humans have emanated while being there. So the feelings became imprinted into the walls, into the items that were placed there. It's not that those spots were sacred in and of themselves. Yes, sometimes there are alignments in the grounds that facilitate this energetically, but mostly it results from the humans and what they were feeling when they entered into such a spot.

So, you do the same whenever you go into your physical temple, the room that is yours, or maybe just a corner of a room. This temple is yours, this is your spot to rejuvenate. Maybe this

is the spot where you will cultivate your awareness, and where you cultivate your light body.

Then one could say that this physical location
becomes like a portal. Humans oftentimes think
of a portal like a wormhole where they jump in
with their physical body and come out somewhere
else, including their physical body, and then visit
other worlds. But this is more or less nonsense, it
doesn't work that way.

A portal is an environment that is supportive
for you to open up, that's all. If you create an atmosphere in your physical temple of opening up,
of openness, of clarity, well, then it's so much
easier for you to open up and go beyond the typical human consciousness.

The third temple is your light body. Your light
body! It's much easier to see your light body as a
temple as opposed to your physical body, for the
light body is yours. It is created by a single intent
of yours of having it. It connects you directly with
all that you are, with pure consciousness.

So, being within your light body will naturally
give you a feeling of awe, of how wonderful creation is in its entirety, even including separation.

So we have already three temples: your physical body, a physical location, and then your light
body.

We also need a kind of temple in the non-physical where you can go with your light body. And

this is what we will create today. This is what we will create today in a very special location!

I will play some music.

*

(*Music plays*)

Take on a body posture of clarity as you have become accustomed to. A posture of openness, of awe. Again, you are about to do the highest a human can do. You go beyond separation, and be it just for moments – what higher could there be? *You are coming home!* So, open up.

First, become aware of our gathering that we have right now, for you might say it takes place in a special dimension that we created on the fly. You created it on the fly when you logged in to the Zoom meeting, and then went into your special mode of "gathering." We gather in the non-physical. You are spread out all over the world with your physical bodies, but our gathering takes place in the non-physical.

So take some time and sense the others; just sensing.

When a human goes into the non-physical, he or she usually tries to *see* images, to *perceive structures*. And then he doesn't, and complains, "There are none! There is nothing visual!" And then they are disappointed and say, "Oh, I didn't do it right. What should I do? Should I just make this up? But even making it up doesn't really

180

work." But actually, in the non-physical, how could there be images? *There are none!*

Every image you might have in the non-physical is made up by the human part of your consciousness, and there is nothing wrong with that! But you need to realize that the images are *always* coming from you. It is "real," but it is real *only for you.* It's not a shared experience like you have in the physical, where you can agree upon physical objects and their size and what they look and feel like. Here in the non-physical, it's not about seeing or touching, it's about sensing and letting go of the need to perceive structures. This is a huge challenge, but you will slowly, slowly get used to it.

Nevertheless, sometimes it's helpful for a human to either consciously or unconsciously produce images of what you sense, without getting stuck in those images. So, you might well imagine or sense the humans in this gathering as, say, light bubbles, or as anything you like. Just know that every representation you come up with is produced by *you.* However, what's behind it *is* real. The entities *are* real!

So, roam around, greet the others in a non-physical way. How do you do that? Oh, you project the greeting outward, as a feeling, "Welcome, nice to meet you once again!"

Twenty humans are gathered here in this special dimension, and it is safe here! It is safe. No one can intrude. We created this dimension implicitly by intent. Oh, if others come across these recordings later, they can join in. You might even feel some of them right now. They are, in a way, invited. They know where to go. They have an invitation by means of this recording.

So, is this dimension or this place where we are meeting similar to a physical room? Well, if you so choose. Is it unlimited in its extensions? Well, if you so choose. Is it spatial at all? Well, if you so choose. All of this is up to you, for we are meeting in the non-physical.

As you go out into the non-physical, it will oftentimes be a bit challenging to go back to the human-only form. Therefore, just as you have a physical place where you can relax and rejuvenate, we are now going to build a temple in the non-physical. Each one of you will build one for yourself. It will be a special place; a temple where you can rest after you ventured out to experience the highest consciousness; a place to relax from human mass consciousness, to integrate, and to open up.

We will build this temple of yours in a very special place that I call *borderland*; borderland.

Imagine all the worlds of separation. Imagine they are all contained in a bubble that floats in pure consciousness. Again, I have to use human images. A bubble is of course spatial and it floats. But let's go with this image. Imagine that all the worlds of separation are contained in a bubble, and the physical universe that you inhabit is also a small bubble within that bubble, a tiny spot within separation.

In a way, you are the pure consciousness that is all around this bubble. You are aware of yourself and of the bubble. It's like you are holding the bubble in your hand, like we did the with the cosmic mudra holding planet Earth.

Become aware of Earth inside the bubble. Now, from within this bubble, go outward towards the surface of the bubble. Note that this going outward is not a question of moving in space, but of subtlety in awareness. Your awareness becomes finer and finer. You allow yourself to be in borderland, on the surface of the bubble, right between the worlds of separation and pure consciousness. You come here without a form; just as a presence; as beingness.

Now, by intent, build your temple. You can imagine it and give it a form, or you can just *know* it is there.

You might imagine it for instance as a light sphere, and you are in the center of it; or as a wonderful room.

It's just yours. It's taking care of you. All intents are instantly reflected! You can have any color that you like, you can sense music if you like, you can create or place beautiful objects here.

This is your place in the borderland. It is safe here. Nobody can intrude here. You might invite others, but nobody can come in without you allowing it.

Get comfortable here.

You might change your temple, for instance, into a normal room that a human would inhabit. Why not? You can imagine you have a human form sitting in a chair, looking at a fireplace. It's all up to you. Your temple responds instantly, and it is real – for you! And that's what counts.

Your temple is built in borderland for a reason. It is a spot where you can relax after you have ventured out into the Third Round of Creation, and before going back into separation.

Therefore, we add two doors to your temple: one door facing the worlds of separation – figuratively leading into the bubble of separation; and one door facing the Third Round of Creation, pure consciousness. Imagine these doors.

It's so beautiful out here, because you can sense the Third Round of Creation. It's so close! It's so close, and actually, we are going to have an excursion there right now; a field trip, so to speak. So, slowly open the door to the Third Round of Creation. Oh, I use various terms for it; sometimes, the Third Round of Creation, sometimes pure consciousness, and sometime Utopia, the no-place.

So, open the door and sense what's out there. Just stand at the threshold of the door and sense. Fortunately, we have desensitized your physical body by means of the Light Body Exercise. That was a good preparation, for the energies here are very, very intense. If you were not used to it, you would run away. But your physical vessel is prepared, your consciousness is prepared. However, you still need to be careful. If you go out there and stay too long, it can become very hard for you to come back. And there's nobody who could bring you back or would bring you back, for it's all your choice. *It's always only your choice!* Where do you want to stay? Where do you want to go?

Good. Now, slowly step out of your door into Utopia, the no-place. Oh, this is beyond form. How could form be in the no-place? Here it's all about sensing and knowing – the knowingness of isness.

Some of you might hear a welcome from other entities that are here. They are in awe. They know what is going on. But they will not interfere. They will not come close unless you come close, for they know about your challenges.

It's difficult to describe with words what is going on here. Here we have undistorted creation; creation that does not rely on the principle of separation.

For a human, this is hard to imagine, but you can feel it. This is what I call true creation.

A creation that goes on and on, that is not temporary. Yet, it's not getting stuck, because it is growing all the time. It's not getting stuck at all.

That is why I use the term *expanding perfection*. It is perfect! Nothing is missing; nothing is lacking, but it's not static either.

Many humans fear that once they are in this kind of existence, in Utopia, they fear it's boring, because they assume nothing ever happens here. But nothing, nothing, nothing could be further from the truth! Here you have true creation, and you share it. That is what you do as a creator. That's what even every human does when he or she creates: they want to share their creation with others, the song, or the poem. They want to share their joy! You hear a joke, you want to share it.

Same here; true creation, and you share. It's shared immediately!

There is no need to create in order to "prove yourself," or "to defend yourself" – it's the pure joy of the creator. Even though you have no form and you are not here as a human, you might breathe it in. And it goes directly into the physical body that is sitting somewhere in this bubble in your universe on a planet called Earth. The physical body can relate to this.

Good. Now, slowly go back into your temple. You can come here as often as you like, but again I warn you: do not stay too long, unless you want to stay forever! Go back into your temple, and close the door. This is symbolic.

Right next to that door that leads to Utopia, create a window. Create a window, an opening; a window into Utopia. This reminds you always where you are when you are here.

Whenever you come here and then go back into your human condition, you bring something with you. Oh, it's not that you stuff your pockets or fill up a tank with fluid light and carry it into the human realm, no. You bring a knowingness of who you truly are; an intensified knowingness of who you truly are: you are an unlimited being beyond any form! You are a being that returns to the world of separation out of empathy and compassion to inspire those who choose to follow in your footsteps.

Whenever you go back from here, you bring clarity, you bring lucidity with you. You make the dream of separation more and more lucid. You become more and more a conscious actor in it.

This is your fourth temple. You don't want to rush back, when you've been so far out. If you would rush directly into your human body it would be very difficult, so instead of doing that, you pause here, you rest. You rest, you integrate, you adjust. You make the conscious choice to go back to your physical body to realize the dream of embodied ascension.

Now, once again become aware of your physical body and simultaneously be aware of the light body residing in your temple in borderland. Now let these two images meld, like slides you overlay. It's just a shift in consciousness, a shift in your perspective.

And here we are: in a moment of embodied ascension!

It doesn't matter how long it lasts. It's a dream come true! You can even say it's a dream within a dream that brought you out of the dream come true.

In a way, borderland is everywhere; it only depends on your awareness. You can go into a grocery store, and know that you are walking in borderland. Why? Because you can simultaneously be in and beyond separation. Being in borderland means you are *in* the dream, yet you know that you are not *of* the dream. And in this transitioning phase, your four temples help you to stabilize this knowingness.

At some point, you will go beyond the temples, but right now they are helpful. They are helpful tools, and there's no reason to reject helpful tools.

Now, I once again remind you of the homework challenge. First thing in the morning, when you get up, go into your physical temple and cultivate your awareness. Then become aware of the tones, in your belly, in your chest, and in your crown. Then continue with cultivating your light body.

Do this the first thing in the morning. And there's a reason for it! There's a reason, why in all the traditions the monks, or whatever they call themselves, get up early in the morning. It is because at that point in time, everything is fresh and the doors to the unconscious are wide open. You are still in the in-between mode – in-between your personal dreams and physical reality. When you then bring clarity and awareness into that, oh, you

188

clear up the unconscious! Suddenly, you can understand what you just dreamt about, and then you can let it go.

Thus, the early morning hours are precious, use them. That's the challenge.

It was again wonderful to be with a group of humans traveling so far out, yet it was just a shift in consciousness. However, so few humans are capable and willing to do it. That's why there was the awe from the other side, from the entities that saw you standing at the doorstep of your temple in the non-physical. They know what is going on, and they are with you in their very own way, just as I am.

I am Althar the Crystal Dragon. Have a good week.

*

Joachim: So, I realize my background picture is back, so we did *something*! If that is not proof, then I don't know what proof is!

Participant 1: Your background picture was superb – the borderland.

Joachim: *(laughing)* Yes, that's true. It's flexible. Now we're back in boring North Sea land. *(the background picture now shows the North Sea)*

Participant 1: Well, I'm still on the edge of borderland, looking at you!

Joachim: Wow!

Any remarks, any questions? Any sharings about experiences you might have had out there?

Participant 2: Does anyone else get really hungry after this?

Joachim: Yes, please give a sign, who gets hungry? *(most participants raise their hand)*

Participant 2: I get so hungry!

Joachim: That's s typical reaction.

Participant 2: What is that?

Joachim: I can tell you from experience – hunger is good. If you are drawn to alcohol instead, you should be a bit careful. That's what happened to me oftentimes. But it's the body, it's the physical body that recognizes, "Oh, consciousness is leaving, but I want to survive. And how do I do that? I better make myself noticeable; feed me, stuff me, so consciousness grounds itself in me!"

190

It's eating, it's drinking, it's sex. It's the nature of biology calling out for you, "Be with me!" Actually, it's a good sign, but it's a bit annoying also. I wouldn't say, you get used to it, but you can try not to eat too much afterwards. You never really get used to it.

Well, I'm beyond the alcohol thing. I remember the early times, when I had more like flash experiences, it was really difficult for me and I needed to ground myself, so I took the whiskey. Since then, I don't drink whiskey anymore, because one time, it was just too much. Now I can't even smell it. Bah, put it away. But it's natural. (*Someone is laughing.*) That's not funny! (*laughs*)

Participant 3: I just wanted to say, that's something I've experienced for some months now. I always, always want to eat sugar. Normally, I hate sugar! (*laughter*) So, I think it's what Joachim said, we have to ground ourselves again.

Participant 2: Yeah, right now, I'm craving a burger, and I don't really eat meat!

Joachim: But to be precise, I don't say you have to. I say the body cries out for it. And, well, you can play along with it for a while, but when it's getting into stuffing mode, relax, take some smaller and fewer bites. Do not give in, because this is also a kind of distraction.

It's like with the Light Body Exercise, when you get too emotional while doing it. That's fine for a while, all the tears and shaking, and body shivers. But at some point, this becomes a hindrance. You can say, "Oh it's good, just some tears." No, after a while, stop it! We go beyond that. It's the same with craving food afterwards. Take care of your physical body. Of course, it has to adjust. Is it a must? Well, maybe it is for you to get grounded again, but try to stay open at the same time, if that is possible for you. Sooner or later, it *is* possible. Don't become the victim of your body, for it would continue eating, eating, eating. The body tells you that eating is better than doing the crazy stuff out there! So, be wise when stuffing your body.

Participant 3: I take long walks in the woods, and then it vanishes.

Joachim: You mean while eating sugar?

Participant 3: (*laughter*) No, I stop then, that's what stops me.

Participant 2: Chocolate, bon bons, and walking!

Participant 3: By the way, it's just M. A friend of mine did the zoom thing for me and he thought it funny to say Gold M. because it's his nickname for me, but....

Joachim: It's a beautiful name, why don't you keep it?

Participant 3: Because of the color of my hair, he always said this to me.

Joachim: I sense something there, but I don't go into it.

Participant 3: Oh no, okay. M. is okay. But just do as you like.

Participant 1: I think it's really amazing though, that I took in what you said sessions earlier about us on this screen – and the connection we have, which has been spoken of, but really not spoken of in depth. And I truly respect there being an amazing connection with us, and so for us to know you are Gold M., seems rather curious to me.

Participant 3: (laughter) Okay, okay. We keep it simple.

Participant 1: I presume we're ancient family together. Being ancient family, I guess we knew you as gold!

Participant 4: I just want to thank you. That was simply wonderful for me. That's the most peaceful I've ever been in a meditation, so thank you all. Thank you. I'm still there…

Joachim: (*laughter*) If you want to check out, don't do it before the last session, alright? We have to stick together here at least another five weeks.

Participant 1: We'll come after you if you leave!

Joachim: Yeah, we'll pull you back.

Participant 4: For most of my life, I thought peace was too boring, now I am getting a sense of how enjoyable and wonderful it is.

Joachim: Yes. That's one of the sad stories spreading here and there. I don't know why some people are saying peace or enlightenment is boring. Then others take it as an excuse to stay here and become the superstar of separation, or they even try to combine "the best" of both worlds, but that's just not working. It's a fallacy.

I always say, you have to go completely out of separation first, and then you can come back, then it's kind of real. If you stay here and pretend you are out there also, well, you are just making it up. It doesn't work that way – at least that's how I get it. Maybe it works for some, but I cannot really see how that could be.

Okay, let's close the session. Have a wonderful week.

I am not responsible for the homework challenge of course, it's somebody else, right? I do it anyway, so it's no problem for me!

So see you next week and great that you are here!

Oh, we need to wave. Don't forget to wave I need the photo… okay, cheese! Okay, ciao.

7. Lucid Perception

We have a lot on the plate for today, so let's just start! And we start out as usual, with cultivating the awareness. So, take on the posture of the master. You're used to it by now. Today it's very important that you maintain that posture even when Althar comes in.

So, straighten your backbone, stretch your backbone. As you do so, the chin comes in a little bit, which again stretches your neck. Then the energy can flow freely. Push the head towards the sky. As you stretch your backbone, your shoulders can relax and fall a little bit backwards.

Like last week I ask you to place the left hand into the right so that the middle fingers overlap and the thumbs touch each other very lightly. Then you place your hands in your lap so that the little fingers touch your belly, and the thumbs are right below your navel.

Close your eyes three quarters, do not focus on anything with your vision, and become aware of your breath. You are breathing in and out through your nose; the mouth is closed, the tongue touches the roof of the mouth, and as you breathe, allow your belly just to follow gravity. Let it totally relax.

As you are simply aware of your breath, the breath finds its natural rhythm. The breathing frequency is decreasing, yet you breathe deeper. Also, the in breath is not as long as the out breath.

Include both of your legs in your awareness. Become totally aware of your legs.

Feel the weight that is resting on your feet.

Now feel the weight that is pressing on your buttocks.

Feel into your hands, and feel again the light touch of your thumbs against each other; a light touch, no tension there. The thumbs are horizontal – they are a perfect mirror of your inner awareness.

Include your arms in your awareness, your shoulders, and your entire chest.

Feel the breath moving your chest as it's going in and out.

Now include your belly.

Feel once again into your thumbs. Did their position change? If so, no problem, just readjust them. Let them touch each other lightly. Keep them positioned horizontally, just as you keep your back bone straight.

Now include your throat in your awareness; your tongue.

(long pause)

Include your mouth, and nose, eyes, forehead, the skin of your head, and the crown in your awareness.

Once again feel into your thumbs, and specifically become aware of the bones in your thumbs; the bones. How do you do that? Well, you place your awareness right there. You might picture it internally. And then you open up! Let your awareness fill the bones of your thumbs.

It feels a bit weird, because one assumes the bones are not really alive, but they are. And they respond to awareness.

Now let your awareness sink into all of your fingers; into the bones of all of your fingers. How would your life be without your fingers, if they wouldn't respond to your intents?

Good. Now let go of all of this body awareness, and just observe. Open up totally to every sensation that comes in, and just take note of it. Whatever comes up, take note of it. Do not follow it, do not chase it, and do not judge it. It arises, you observe it, and you let it go.

The moment you realize you are drawn into your thoughts, emotions, or feelings, you come back to your body awareness. You stretch your backbone, feel the touch of your thumbs, and then you open up again to pure observation.

Take note how all your body functions relax. The breathing has calmed down, the mind has calmed down. And what did you do? Well, nothing. You stopped doing.

Now I want you to become aware of the space that your body occupies; the space. That's interesting, right? The space is not the body itself, so you have no direct sensation or feeling of this space, but you can connect to it. You exist in space, and without space, your body couldn't be here. And this can be felt.

Now become aware of the space that is right around your physical body; that's close to your physical body. How do you do that? Well you just extend your awareness.

Actually, if you look into matter, into the atoms, you realize that they consist mostly of empty space. So the space outside of your body and the space within your body are totally connected. There is no boundary in any way. Feel that connection.

Same with the air that you breathe; it's within your lungs and it is outside.

Now let the awareness of the space in and outside of you extend outwardly; make it larger. Fill out the whole room you are sitting in right now. You are totally connected with this space.

Now extend beyond the room and include the house where that room resides.

Extend your awareness of space more and more until you include all of Earth; the space that planet Earth is contained in.

And of course there is no reason to limit yourself to just this tiny Earth. Space is all over the universe that you inhabit. So, include all of that. Be aware of all of this space; the quality of space. And no matter what happens in this universe, you can let it go! If a sun collapses somewhere in outer space, well, take note, let it go.

Good. Now come back to the dimensions of your physical body. It's just a shift in perspective.

The space is the same. The quality of the space is the same. It's up to you how far you want to extend outwards. Of course when you are living your daily life, it's practical to just be in your physical body and in a surrounding that you can somehow relate to as a physical being. Apart from that, you are totally free.

Now place your awareness into your Hara and become aware of the tone that is emanating from there, the deep sound.

Also become aware of the tone that is emanating from your chest; a higher pitched tone.

Include the tone that is emanating from your crown, a nearly inaudible tone.

And now sense into a spot that is maybe a meter above your head; there is also a tone emanating. A very, very high pitched tone that is way beyond the human hearing range – but you can tune into that. And as you do, whoa, the doors open wide, the doors in consciousness.

Imagine a sine wave representing a tone. The frequency of a deep sound is low. The higher the sound gets, the higher its frequency. Now what happens if you go as high as possible? If you "squeeze" this sine wave? The sound gets higher and higher. The frequency approaches infinity. If you imagine a drawing of it, the curve looks like a filled rectangle. But in a way, every tone is contained in this inaudible sound, this impossible sound.

(long pause)

Even though you are simultaneously aware of multiple sounds, your body, and maybe even still aware of the space, relax. You do not have to juggle with various phenomena. No! You simply come back to your natural state!

So, stay in this awareness while I play some music and we will invite Althar in.

*

(*Music plays*: "Familiar", *Agnes Obel*)

I am Althar the Crystal Dragon.

I have to say I love beautiful music, just as I love beauty. And I always remind you that whatever you perceive as beautiful is indeed a reminder of the true beauty that is already within. Nevertheless, a beautiful song, like we have just heard, is a wonderful reminder! But do not get stuck in the beauty that comes from separation. The beauty of true creation that awaits you exceeds everything you can even imagine within separation.

Today I'd like you to join our "on the fly created meeting dimension" in your light body! So, just get in communion with your true self, hold the intent to have a light body, and then bring it here. And I want you to have your light body in a human shaped form. It doesn't mean it has to look precisely as you do, you can make it as beautiful as you like, but let it have two arms, two legs, a head, and two eyes. Also bring a chair with you, so you can sit comfortably with your light body. Not that you need a chair to sit, but right now, for this set up, a chair is good.

We arrange the chairs in a huge circle. A huge circle for we have a couple of guests today, very special guests. You might feel them already. I brought a few friends of mine; a few dragons. Old buddies of mine, and I jokingly call us *The Crystal Gang*. So, today we are not dealing with the dragons you have already bonded with, say, your personal dragon, but we bring in different dragons. I have one for each and every one of you.

There is one specialty with dragons in general: we have no gender. But the humans perceive us typically in a human gender. Well, this comes of course deep from their unconscious, from their wishes and also from their fears. So, if you ask your peers in the group here if they have assigned a gender to their dragon, then I would say that all the females have female dragons and all the males have male dragons. There are always some exceptions, but very few will go with a, say, "neutral" dragon. It usually has certain gender characteristics.

The dragon who will come to you is exactly the opposite of the one that you would typically prefer. If you are adjusted to, say, a female dragon, then the dragon that comes to you will emphasize his male characteristics, so that you perceive the dragon as a male dragon – and vice versa for the other gender. Actually, you might say that dragons are truly "diverse" as you say today. We could emphasize each and every aspect of ourselves, and we could emphasize all of our, say, "gender aspects" simultaneously, but then we would just be a blazing light and wouldn't be of much help for you today.

So, take on the posture of the master, for you are soon meeting a dragon that you have never encountered before. Today, they come in as huge creatures! Ten times the size of an elephant, to give you an idea. Let them come in. They are landing right now in the circle we have formed here, and one dragon comes directly to you – feel that.

No need to fear anything. As you know, the dragons are compassionate. Well, of course their clarity might cause some anxiety, but you know that the dragons never act on this. Whatever appears to happen is all within you – the dragon simply reflects it back to you.

Feel how the dragon lowers his head and is looking right into your eyes, into the eyes of your light body. Its head may be half a meter away from you. You know that the dragon sees everything! You cannot hide anything from the dragon. You might hide things from yourself or you might pretend they don't exist, but the dragon sees it all! At the same time, the dragon doesn't really care. It overlooks all these details, all these story details that you carry with you. The dragon sees you as you truly are: *an unlimited being!* An unlimited being in the disguise of a limited human! Yes, you are sitting here in a light body, but nevertheless you are still very much connected to the flesh and bones of your human body.

So, face your dragon, do not try to hide anything.

I brought my friends with me, because today we have to talk about a very serious topic for which I need your full attention. And the dragons will not allow you to run away.

All the entities of the second round of creation, including you, share one characteristic: *they are all addicts!* Addicts! Each and every entity! Feel into that – an addict.

What is an addict? An addict craves a substance, something from the outside; craves it and craves it, and when he gets his substance, there is a short period of relaxation, a very short period. And soon after, the next dose has to come, usually a higher dose. If it's not coming, oh then, then you have the monkey, you are struggling for your drug.

You are on this drug not only since the day you were born. You were on this drug since the very moment you entered separation! Now what is this drug? Let the dragon in front of you help you. Feel into yourself. What is this drug that you rely on so heavily?

*

Well, the drug is perception!

You would not exist as a separate being without perception making you believe you are a separate being. It is *only* perception that keeps you in the loop – the eternal feedback loop of separation.

You do not know who you are, but you *perceive.* Therefore, you think that what you perceive constitutes your existence. And should you have no perceptions even for a moment, you get frantic. You don't know who you are any more. Thus, you have to perceive again and again and again.

But as everything in separation is transient, every perception ceases sooner or later, and so does the imagined subject that you believe yourself to be – the ego. The ego is established by perceiving an object "outside" of itself, thereby validating itself to exist on some imagined "inside."

That is what perception does. This is the drug. This is the drug that all entities share. I say that separation and perception cannot exist without each other. They are mutually dependent!

Without perception there wouldn't be separation; without separation there wouldn't be perception.

Hence, it is as difficult to go beyond perception as it is to go beyond separation.

Now, in a linear mindset you might say, "Well, we have a hen and egg problem here. What came first, separation or perception?" But that's not true. We are beyond time! Both came into existence simultaneously. And ever since, they form an eternal feedback loop constituting your ego, and constituting all appearances in separation.

Oh, we've talked about this at length. I started talking about this in "The New Magi," and repeated it here and there. We've talked about it in "The Lucid Dreamer," but perception seems to be, in a way, so natural. Everybody does it. Everybody is on this drug, so where is the point? And at the same time, perception is a bit technical. It's also a bit boring to talk about it, isn't it? However, you have to really grasp the implications! What is perception in essence? What does it do to you?

And just like any normal addict, you might also say, "You know, it's not so bad. I only take it once in a while."

No! No, no, no! You take it in each and every moment, with the exception of maybe one hour when you are in deep sleep, without any dreams. Apart from that, perception is always on, and you are always craving it.

Now, each addict only has a chance to come off his drug if he makes the deep choice to do so. You can offer him therapies of all kinds, but unless the addict makes the deep choice to get off the needle, it will not happen. He will always find a reason to return to his drug addicted life.

So, what you have to do, what you can do right now, is to make this deep choice. And the dragon right in front of you is there to help you, for that dragon represents the *Eye of Suchness*. The Eye of Suchness is a way to perceive without creating illusions, without solidifying the belief in separation, without falling prey to a drug.

But before you make the choice, here in this, well, sacred setting, be aware that making the choice in itself does not change a thing! However, only when you make the choice can the cleansing begin, can the drug slowly, slowly, be let out of your system. And even though you might choose the Eye of Suchness now, you will most certainly suffer a relapse! You will fall back into the habits of perception, because you have done so since the beginning of separation. Relapses are normal. Thus, you have to make the choice again, and again, and again!

Here, now, you can make that choice for yourself; a deep choice. You can express the deep desire and the deep wish to go beyond, no matter how long it takes to get off the drug. No addict knows how long it might take for him. If you have been smoking for thirty years, well, for some the addiction could be gone the next day. And others need weeks and weeks, and years. With alcohol or heroin, it's much harder, but you *can* do it. As soon as you feel the urge to go back to the drug or you catch yourself in being back in the drug, you just make the choice again – and throw the needle away, instantly. That is what I call choosing the Eye of Suchness.

Now, before you make that choice, let me summarize what it means to choose the Eye of Suchness when you are in your physical environment as a human. We might dissect this into four steps.

First comes step one, the wake-up call, the remembrance. You are in the midst of something in your daily life, whatever it is, and suddenly you get that wake-up call from within. You realize, "I'm *not* what perception leads me to believe." That's the remembrance. It comes from, say, your divine spark. The spark from your true self, pure consciousness, true reality, that can never be veiled. It's always there. It might be hidden for a long time, but sooner or later it shines through. And when it shines through you remember, "I am not what perception leads me to believe!"

And then comes the second step: clarity. You know: "Nothing that I perceive is real. It is dream-like. It is distorted by the interpretations of my past, of my history, of my wishes, desires, and fears. Therefore, I do not need to cling to it!" That is clarity.

And then comes the third step: it's the choice. You choose the Eye of Suchness instead of the Eye of Separation. And by doing so, you understand that you perceive illusions, but you stop believing in their reality! You do not make them real anymore! Therefore, you do not make the perceiving subject real anymore. That is the choice.

With that choice comes the fourth step: the realization that there is a reality beyond separation! I am unlimited! I am All-That-Is! This is the fourth step.

That is what I mean by choosing the Eye of Suchness.

From a didactical point of view, it makes sense to explain it with these four steps. In reality, when you get used to it, it takes just an instant and it all comes together. You get that wake-up call, and then you remember, "Oh, I am All-That-Is, no matter what perception is trying to tell me!" And just as you come back to your awareness when you cultivate your awareness, you will come back to this realization when you choose the Eye of Suchness.

So, now, in this sacred circle with all the witnesses and the dragon facing you right now, what do you choose?

And you are not urged to do anything. You can come back to this at a later time. But make a choice within if you want to go off the drug, no matter how long it takes, or if you want to continue playing in separation.

*

Choosing the Eye of Suchness is like wielding a sword that instantly cuts off all illusions. It's the sword of clarity. It's always at your disposal.

Now, see the dragon in front of you with your Eye of Suchness, and feel what happens.

Well, the dragon now loses its male or female characteristics. They are not important any more, you overlook these attributes. When two entities see each other with the Eye of Suchness, they join in Suchness. They realize, "We are not two!" You see, I don't say, "They are one." No, they are *not two*. Feel this with the dragon that is facing you right now. Not two.

Whenever you choose the Eye of Suchness, you choose the dragon within that you already are. You choose clarity. You choose realization. You choose the utmost acceptance of All-That-Is for you *are* All-That-Is.

Really understanding perception is difficult, precisely because it's *not* difficult to understand the underlying principles. You can explain the mechanics of perception to a ten year old child! What *is* difficult is what follows when you take your discoveries seriously! When you stop perceiving, that is when there's a real problem. That is when the fear of the addict comes through, not knowing any more "Who or what am I?" As an addict, at least you have a reason to get up in the morning! You crave perceptions to feed you, to keep you alive as a separate being.

But the principle of perception is very, very simple. Just as everything is very simple the deeper you go into consciousness. At their core, the building blocks, the mechanics of separation, are very, very simple.

Now, I want to make a side note to plant a seed. The dragon in front of you initially emphasized a polarity that was opposing you. Let's say you are a female, so that dragon took on the male characteristics. If two such entities, if two such energies join in suchness, they transmute into what I call *fluid light*. They transcend the polarities. They let go of them.

Fluid light is the basis for what I call true creation.

Feel into that... going beyond the polarities. No fights anymore. No antagonisms – just suchness expressing in suchness.

Good, now I want you to bid farewell to the dragon in front of you... in suchness.

The dragon bows to you, for he or she knows what you are doing. You are here on behalf of all of existence to go beyond perception. So, he's in awe, she is in awe; we are all in awe of the humans!

And with that, the Crystal Gang leaves, and it's only me who remains here to talk to you.

*

We just had a pretty intense experience with the Eye of Suchness and the Crystal Gang. After an intense experience, it's generally good to move a bit, so we will conduct an experiment: I want you to dance with your light body! And as you do, realize that the light body responds to each and every one of your intents. So, whatever you intend to do, whatever move you want to make, you can do it. And I really want you to go wild!

Maybe you remember some great night where you were out dancing, maybe even drug induced. You went wild, sweated, and just let go of all control. Now, here you can do the same, but you can also go far beyond this type of dancing. By intent, you can grow a thousand arms and legs and wave them. You can make the most drastic moves with your light body. You can grow to any size; grow to the size of the cosmos, and then shrink to the size of an atom, all in the rhythm of the music. And I want you to do exactly that. I want to see you sweating in your light body. So, do not hold back, and let the music inspire you!

(*Music plays:* "Song of the Golden Dragon", *Estas Tonne)*

*

So, you're still here! Ah! What a good shake off. All the belief systems were rattled, and all the perception processes were, let's say, readjusted. Now, if your chair still exists, if you didn't crush it in your dance, just sit down on it. And if it did vanish, well, create a new one. Relax, sit down. Isn't it fantastic what you can do without a physical body? Dancing was never easier, was it?

Now, I want to continue the discussion about perception. As you sit here in our meeting dimension on your wonderful chair of light, also become aware of the room your physical body is sitting in right now. Become aware of the physical objects surrounding you in that room. Sense them or imagine them as consisting of soft white light.

Also, become aware of your physical body. You know you are sitting here in this light chair, in our meeting dimension, yet become aware of your physical body on planet Earth. You see it from the outside, and seen from this perspective, it is not that special. Your body is not that different from the chair, or couch, or bed you are sitting on right now, is it? It's not so different.

In the beginning segment, when you were cultivating your awareness, you became aware of the space in and around you. Right now I want you to repeat that. Become aware of the space in your room, your physical room where your body is sitting right now. This space contains all of the objects in the room including your physical body.

Now, *be* that space. *Be* the one who provides the space for all of this.

Know that you are the space right now. *Know* that all the objects are within you. Now I ask you to see these objects simultaneously from the perspective of your physical eyes. So, in a way you are getting two images, one showing you the white soft light objects, and then you have your more or less "normal" perception. Two images, but do not superimpose them, do not overlay them. Leave them in their respective domains.

When you first start doing this, it feels a bit stressful, unnatural. However, it's the very same as becoming aware of multiple body parts at the same time. In the beginning, this is also a bit stressful, unusual, and unnatural. But as you practice it, you realize, "I'm going back to normal!" It *is* natural to be aware of multiple things. It *is* natural to be aware of all and at the same time be aware of something from a specific perspective. Just as it is natural for you to see and hear simultaneously.

What you are doing right now is what I call *lucid perception*. It is a way of perceiving, but it brings in the clarity, the lucidity. As you get used to it, you undo the most distorting factor of the perception process, namely the process that establishes you as a perceiving subject. Why is that? Well, because you are simultaneously aware of All-That-Is.

And All-That-Is is actually all within you. You are the space right now. You are the physical body in that space. The body sits within you.

You see, perception constantly creates a contradiction with your innate knowingness that all is within, because when a human hears or feels "all is within," he relates it to his body. And how could that be? Well, this is not what is meant. "All is within" means: *all is within your consciousness, including your physical body.*

As you apply lucid perception, you get rid of the most momentous distortion of perception: *you stop making the perceiving subject real!* You just stop doing so, naturally. You do not force yourself out of existence. No! You just see things as they truly are.

It is as if you are the sky, and there are clouds floating in it. You are aware of the clouds within you. At the same time, you can project yourself into one such cloud and perceive the sky from that perspective. You can perceive yourself and you can perceive the apparent "other" clouds. If you then forget about the sky, and suddenly believe that you are a cloud, then you are back in separation. That's the distorted perception process. However, as long as you are aware that everything happens within you, that you are just as much the sky as you are the projection into the cloud, you are not trapped anymore by separation!

So, lucid perception is a fundamental change in the perception process!

It is a fundamental change. I really want you to grasp the significance of this, and that's why we had this, how to say, this dramatic appearance of the Crystal Gang. Perception sounds boring and not that sexy. Not as sexy as the Third Round of Creation! But as far as embodied ascension goes, well, you do need lucid perception! Otherwise chances are that you just fall back into the ways of the old perception addicts, forgetting about everything, being on the needle once again.

Lucid perception emphasizes the All-Is-Within-knowingness. As this sinks in deeper and deeper into you, the dream of separation lightens up. It's not that heavy anymore. And this is where lucid perception and choosing the Eye of Suchness meet. In the end result, well they are the same. You are All-That-Is, yet you can perceive from a specific perspective.

Choosing the Eye of Suchness is more coming from within the dream and wielding the sword of clarity once again, to follow your wake up call. Lucid perception is more coming from the absolute and then going back into separation.

So, I use two terms mostly for didactical purposes. But in the end, they lead to the same result: you see things as they truly are.

Throughout this whole session, we brought in many levels of information, starting with the first segment, cultivating the awareness, up to this very point. So, you might want to go into this again and repeat it. Many, many levels of information – not everything has been said explicitly.

I also remind you of the homework challenge. First thing in the morning, when you wake up, do not argue with yourself, just get up, grab your coffee or whatever you need, and cultivate your awareness. Then hear the sounds – in your Hara, your chest, your crown, and above your head. And finally, cultivate your light body. How long should you do it? That's up to you, but there's no reason to not go really into it.

And then, whenever it occurs to you throughout the day, when you get that wake-up call, choose the Eye of Suchness, and switch to lucid perception. It doesn't matter how long it lasts, just become aware of the alternate view of existence. Become aware of all the formations in consciousness that you see as white light. All of this is within you. That is what you remember when you choose the Eye of Suchness and apply lucid perception – *all is within*.

I have to say, I am very proud of this group. We have come very, very far. I'm just scanning history… but I cannot see a tradition or anything where things were expressed in this way. It's very much adapted to the contemporary human, to their understanding. We do not bother with deities or gods or whatever. No, it's just you, a bit of more or less easy to understand analysis, coming to the right conclusions, and then it's you being brave enough to put the insights to practice.

You know what? This is what changes the blueprint, the template: *Bringing in lucid perception, applying it, making it normal – this is the easing of the way out.*

I am Althar, a proud Crystal Dragon! I'm already looking forward to seeing you again next week. Good night.

*

Joachim: So, I see all of you are still here. You have at least two arms! I don't know the number of legs that you have! But two arms is a good start.

(*chuckles; some are waving their hands*)

A couple of fingers also!

I need a bit of fluid light. (*sipping water*)

So, the funny thing for me was to see how everyone started smiling when they were dancing. That was nice to see! Before, everyone made such a stern face, and then suddenly all were more or less grinning.

Okay, so I don't assume there is much need to talk right now, which is usually a good sign. So, with that we close the session.

Thank you! See you next week!

8. Light World and Feeling Realities

Welcome everybody!

So, I see you can hear me. I *see* you can *hear* me; that's weird! As usual, we have a lot on the plate today, so we start out immediately with cultivating the awareness.

As always, take on the position of the master, the position of clarity, and royalty. Stretch the backbone, pull the chin in a little bit, and press the head against the sky, or your ceiling, depending on where you are. Shoulders are relaxed, they fall a bit backwards. You create the cosmic mudra by placing the left hand in your right, the fingers are overlapping each other and the thumbs are horizontal and touch each other lightly.

Good.

The mouth is closed. The tip of the tongue touches the roof of the mouth and the backside of the upper teeth. You breathe in and out naturally through the nose.

The eyes are three quarters closed; just leave them a little bit open so some light comes in. Then it's harder for you to fall asleep or follow your dreams.

Now, become aware of your feet; both feet simultaneously.

Include your lower legs in your awareness... your knees... and your upper legs.

As you breathe, feel how you also breathe through the skin of your legs. It sounds weird, but it's possible. You can breathe with all the pores of your skin. And as you do, you can sense how the legs are energized.

Now include your hands in your awareness, and also breathe through your hands.

Become aware of your buttocks, your genitals, and yes, you can also breathe through them.

Include both of your arms in your awareness.

Now include your belly and your chest. Feel how they both move a little bit as you breathe. Also breathe through the skin of your belly, your chest, and your arms.

Include your shoulders in your awareness, and your throat.

And now all of your head – specifically, become aware of your eyes, and breathe through them.

Now the same with your ears; feel them, and breathe through them.

And now your crown; feel it, and breathe through it.

Now breathe through every pore in your skin, and through your nose. Whole body breathing – feel what this does to you.

It's a total rejuvenation. If you are tired at some point in your daily life and you are used to this kind of body awareness, well, do it; become aware of your full body, breathe in through your whole body, and wonders will happen. Actually, if you are very proficient, you even have to be a bit careful not to bring in too much energy, because you might get high from it.

Good. Now let go of the body awareness and just open up to pure observation. Be totally open. Observe what occurs inside you and outside of you. What is presented to you?

However, whatever is presented, you just let it go. You take note, and let go. No associations, no judgments, no nothing.

The moment you realize you are drawn into your thoughts and ideas and dreams, you come back to your posture, a posture of clarity. You readjust your thumbs, your backbone, and your chin. You become aware again of all of your body, and then you change to pure observation.

Now, just like in the last session, I want you to become aware of the space within you and all around you.

As you do, you notice that your awareness is not tied to your body. It can be expanded or it can be more focused. It's totally flexible.

Space is a wonderful analogy for consciousness. Of course, consciousness is beyond space, but for the human understanding, space and consciousness are very similar. Space is always there. It contains everything, it doesn't judge, it doesn't reject. It contains everything beautiful, and everything distasteful; light and dark. You cannot

221

split space, or cut out space out of space. Space doesn't age. That's interesting: everything within space ages, but space itself does not.

So, becoming aware of space is a very good symbolic step to be fully aware of all of consciousness. Consciousness is literally unlimited, it holds everything, and you cannot cut out anything out of it.

It's very, very liberating to be aware of the space as space; not as a visitor of space but as space itself.

Now, where does consciousness end? Is it important? Is there an end to consciousness – some kind of boundary? No, there isn't. No boundary that has been discovered by any entity so far. Maybe there is, but it's unknown if there is one. And I would go so far as to say it is unknowable.

Good, become again aware of your physical body, and feel the sound that emanates from your Hara; the deep humming sound.

Include the sounds emanating from your chest, your crown, and the point about one meter above your crown.

Feel how these sounds of you fill all the space around you.

In case you are intoning these sounds internally, let that go, just hear them. They are already there without you doing anything actively.

As you sense these tones, become aware of your fingers, specifically of the bones of your fingers. And if you tune into them, you will also sense a sound emanating from them; from the bones of your fingers.

Now include your whole skeleton in your awareness, starting from the feet.

Your legs, your backbone, your chest, arms, head... all the bones.

You might picture your skeleton internally. It's a wonder and archaic at the same time. Without the skeleton, how could you really experience physicality, or moving in physicality?

Apart from your teeth, your bones are the hardest matter inside you. This is the matter that you believe yourself to be. And there is a sound emanating from the skeleton.

Can you feel how your inner reality changes as you breathe through all of your body and hear the sounds from your body? It's very different than what you are used to.

Good. Now let go of all of this awareness of the skeleton and the tones and go back to observation once again – pure observation.

Good. I will play some music, and with the music Althar will join us.

*

(*Music plays*: "Always look on the bright side of life", *Eric Idle/Monty Python*)

I am Althar, the Crystal Dragon! I come from the *bright* side of life, and today I will invite you to look at the *light* side of life. So we are taking a big trip, a big journey today, into *light world*. Actually, as we prepared the session for today, we realized that this session in itself could have been split into a whole ten week program. But nevertheless, we decided to put it all into one session, for our aim here is first and foremost to transform much of the knowledge from the Althar material into true experiences for you.

All the topics we will recapitulate today can be found with in-depth discussions in the books, specifically in "Opus Magnum," and "The Lucid Dreamer." Today, it's all about bringing these insights and wisdom into your real experience. And to do so, I invite you to go far beyond the mental, to go into your imagination, to not get stuck in the words I use, or the metaphors I use, or the descriptions I use, but to connect with the knowingness that I attempt to convey.

To facilitate going beyond the mind and into the imagination, we will have music throughout this whole session. I will start this music now and then we will go onto a kind of wild ride.

(*Music plays*)

Good. So, get settled; gather yourself. Take on the posture of clarity, of royalty, and open up to your imagination. Open up wide!

We've spoken a lot about perception in the last weeks. Today we will have a look at what perception actually perceives. To do so, we go back to the very basics, to the beginning of existence in separation, so to speak.

Consciousness has two main characteristics: it can become aware of itself, and it can have intents. Now, if consciousness experiences separation, then we have something that is called pure energy, which is, in a way, consciousness in a crystallized state. This pure energy has the ability to reflect intents. It does so by taking on a specific formation, and then consciousness can become aware of the reflection – or you might say, it perceives the reflection.

The formation that the pure energy takes on is called by me *ousia*. It's an old term that was also used by the Greeks, and others. Many philosophers have used it to express things like beingness or suchness. And therefore, we feel it's a very appropriate term, for ousia together with perception are at the very basis of everything in separation. And the totality of all ousia that exist throughout consciousness in separation is called *light world*.

The term light world in itself is beautiful. However, I have a cautionary note here: *do not confuse true creation with light world!* There is no true creation in the realms of separation, and light world is the fundamental basis for all the worlds and all the experiences in separation.

So, even if you have access to light world, it's not that you suddenly become a better creator or have new means to create. It's not about that. We bring in the topic of ousia and light world to get a deeper understanding of the dream mechanics of separation – how they work out, and how they keep the entities for eons and eons captured in the belief that separation is real.

Contrary to what most humans think, perception does not just present to you a stream of raw data that you then change, transmute, manufacture into an inner image of objects that are related somehow to each other. Perception does way more than give you a stream of details.

In the perception process, you perceive so called *sentiments*. A sentiment is related to a feeling; it is a stimulus for a feeling. For every feeling, we have a corresponding sentiment.

Take a joke for instance. A simple joke is a stimulus for being amused. But just being a stimulus doesn't mean that every perceiver of that joke actually becomes amused. There is no guarantee. Therefore, I say a sentiment is a stimulus. It influences the perceiver, it nudges it a little bit, and sometimes the nudging is enough to trigger the real feeling, but sometimes it goes unnoticed. However, the stimulus will always influence the perceiver a little bit. It's like when the rain falls into the ocean – the ocean doesn't change too much because of the rain drops, but each drop creates its own small waves, and they ripple out and influence the ocean.

An entity conceives itself first and foremost as what it feels in a given moment. If I ask you to feel into yourself, you do not say to yourself, "Well, today I am 1m75, my weight is 80 kg," or anything like that.

No, you automatically assess your feeling state. This feeling state, this "self- feeling" of you, has many, many layers. Right now, you might be very open to high consciousness. Maybe you are a bit excited to hear about the topics we are going to talk about today. At the same time, you might be a bit tired or hungry, or you have body pain here or there. So, there are many, many feelings overlaying in any entity at all times creating their self-feeling. Still, there is a sentiment corresponding to each self-feeling, it's a multilayered sentiment.

The important point is that during the perception process sentiments are exchanged between the perceiver and the ousia, the formation of pure energy. No matter the self-feeling you have at a given moment, when you perceive something, you transmit the corresponding sentiment to the ousia, and the ousia is charged with this sentiment. It's stored there, it's saved there. And when you perceive the ousia, the ousia also sends to you all the sentiments it has stored up so far. So it's a give and take, it's a back and forth between perceiver and ousia. It's a feedback loop, for as you perceive the ousia, you revive it in a way. You have an intent to perceive, and this intent revives the ousia. It solidifies it; stabilizes it. Thus, the ousia is in a constant state of change. Well, we are in separation – nothing is permanent in separation! With each and every perception of an ousia, the sentiment stored there changes. So, there is a constant change in the ousia; a constant change.

Let's give an example that every one of you should be able to relate to. Consider yourself when you were, say, three years old. I would bet that all of you had some favorite doll, or teddy bear, or soft toy. Let's say it was a teddy bear. It was your favorite buddy, not animated, but for you it was as if this teddy bear was alive. It represented something to you – it represented warmth, closeness, friendship, safety, maybe even love. So you held it close when you went to bed at night. It was with you in the same bed and you charged it with that self-feeling of you. Therefore, it reflected it to you, it mirrored it to you. Once it was charged with sentiments, it would be enough to have it close and you would feel immediately better.

That's the story of the teddy bear, and I would bet that some of you have your very first favorite teddy bear or doll or puppet still around somewhere, hidden in some closet. You were not really able to throw it away, to dump it. No, for it represents a precious memory.

This example makes it quite clear that a child does not live in the details that his perception process might present to him, like, what size is the teddy bear, its color, is it of polyester or cotton or plastic or whatever. No. The child lives in his feelings, his emotions, and these are triggered by his teddy bear; stimulated by it. The child lives in a feeling reality, not in a reality of details, facts, and figures.

And this is a general observation, as it is true for every entity in the second round of creation. For every entity, not just for you when you were small child, details play a very, very insignificant role. It's always, always the feelings that make up your current state of being. That's why you say, "I feel tired today," and not "I feel like I'm 1m75 tall today."

Even though you might not have your teddy bear around anymore, well, there are other objects that took on the place of the teddy bear. Maybe you have some photographs of your family, of your partner, your spouse; of a nice location, a holiday, all charged with certain sentiments. They might again stimulate the feelings within you! That's why you have them around. They anchor you in your story and in your place in time.

Now, this understanding has severe consequences. For if it's true that an ousia is created out of an intent, and then is charged with sentiments, this actually means that no ousia has any meaning in and of itself! No ousia whatsoever!

It is always the perceiver giving the meaning to it and deriving a feeling from it!

If an ousia is perceived by many, shared by many, well, then it is charged all the more. So, one might say that a certain spot or object is sacred. But it didn't become sacred because it was created out of the hands of God – unless you call yourself God, which you are of course; but then, every creation you ever made is sacred. Instead, it was charged with sentiments that stimulate a feeling of sacredness.

Thus, no ousia has any value in itself other than the value that you give to it.

This is drastic! This is an understanding that has the capacity to transform you instantly, for why would you hang on to anything in separation if everything is arbitrary? Why, why oh why would an entity try to bring something from separation with him or her into the Third Round of Creation? Why bargain with separation? For your special story? For your special capabilities? It just makes no sense! It just makes no sense.

And with that understanding, the idea often comes that it would be a sacrifice if you let go of anything. But how far from the truth could that be? For how could you sacrifice anything if you let go of limitations? If you become all, then what could you sacrifice other than illusions that weren't real in the first place?

So, it's the feeling realities where the entities live.

Now let's have a deeper look at these feeling realities, specifically at the roles space and physicality play in them. To do so, I want you to consider the game of chess. Chess is of course known by mostly every human on the planet, and as soon as I say the word "chess," an enormous number of sentiments come in. Now, what does it evoke in you, just hearing the term "chess"?

Oh, chess might stand for mental, maybe analytical. Those who are good at chess are smart. Or you might say, "I've never been good at chess, just as I've never been good at mathematics." Chess might be boring, for nothing seems to happen other than two people staring at the chess board, not moving for hours. So the word "chess" is charged with your personal history, your personal sentiments, coming from your past, and it's also charged with sentiments coming from mass consciousness. The world champion in chess is typically a respected person.

Let's have a deeper look into chess. Consider two chess players looking at a position on a chess board. Imagine them, right in front of your inner eye. They are sitting there. Try to see through their eyes. Pick one of those players and see a piece, say, the king. It's a piece on the chess board. And the first thing a chess player associates with the king is, well, fear of death. The king needs to be safe, for if the king is captured, the game is over. So the king is highly charged with sentiment. It needs to be alive, it needs to be protected.

Now, feel into the queen. It's the most powerful piece on the board. That's interesting, right? The queen is female, yet she's the most powerful entity on the board, while the king needs protection. In your normal life, it's typically reversed.

It's somehow felt that the female needs protection, and the king goes out and goes to war for her, for the love of his life. But here on the chess board it's the other way around. But still, the queen knows that she can only live when the king is alive; as soon as the king is dead, the queen is also dead. So, there's a polarity even within the individual pieces of the same color, not just between the opposing colors. You can go through all of these pieces and they have all their specific lives, their specific features.

Then consider the position in general. There's a whole story unfolding; a story of traps, of ambushes, of dominance, of radiation, of threats. This is a full-fledged living reality in the mind of the players. And they are not just looking at this given position, but they are thinking three, four, five, ten moves in advance, depending on how good they are, to see what could happen then. And with every move they make in their inner world, they have to evaluate the new position.

And what does it mean to evaluate a position? Well, it's checking: is the king safe? Did I improve my position? How can I position my individual pieces so that they can attack the other king? This is full of life, and because they cannot calculate to the very end – because there are too many variants – they have to rely on their own history of knowingness, on their gut feeling, on the expertise they've developed over their years of playing.

In the end, they have to go by their feeling, for there is no such thing as an objective evaluation. If one player likes, say, complex positions, well, he favors those. And another player might favor very simple positions where most pieces have been exchanged and you end up with just a king and two pawns!

Thus, the evaluation is highly, highly personal. Those two players, staring at the chess board, they live in a very special world full of life. If you want to express it that way, it's a fight for life and death. Just like separation is, for your body has to be safe with every step you take. No matter how beautiful your plans are, if you fall off the cliff with the next step you take, well, you have made a big mistake.

So, even though both players look at the same position, they experience drastically different feeling realities. They are completely different even though they spring from the same set of pieces standing around on the chess board.

Quite generally you can say: even if two perceivers perceive the same set of ousia, the feeling realities emanating from their perceptions are completely different. It's a bit strange, isn't it?

Now let's have a look at the physicality of this. I asked you to imagine two players sitting at a table with a chess board and of course you imagined some pieces on the board. Now, the pieces could be of wood, of plastic, of stone, of metal. They could have more or less standard forms or weird forms, like they sometimes have. But actually, the physicality of the pieces is absolutely not important. They are just placeholders in the physical for a position in chess that is essentially non-physical. For in essence, a chess position is just a bit of information that tells you on which coordinates a piece is located. It suffices to have that information. You do not need a physical piece.

The physical representation of the pieces is just for the humans to ease their thinking a little bit. However, those who are good at chess, they don't need it. They can play without chess pieces. Just as any computer does; there are no physical pieces around, no. So the physicality of the pieces is irrelevant as the very same feeling reality emerges within a player even without the physical pieces – give or take a few sentiments that may come from the physical objects.

What about space? It appears that the pieces are moving in space on this chess board, but do they? Sure, the players take, say, a pawn and advance it one square, okay. But this is more or less a communication, saying, "I move my pawn from here to there." Thus, the space as such is also not required. And even the chess board, this big square containing the sixty four small squares, it doesn't need to be there. It doesn't need to be arranged as a square, you can split it into sixty four individual squares and throw them somewhere into the universe. It's not important where these squares are located as long as they have the coordinates assigned to them.

So what is this chess position in reality? If you think in terms of ousia, it's just a small amount of plain information – there's a coordinate, occupied by a certain piece, which has a rule attached to it defining where it can move to. That's it, that's the position. And from that come the feeling realities of everybody seeing this chess position.

So, in essence we can strip away the physicality and the space from the game of chess. And actually, it is very much the same with your feeling realities. The physicality and the space, in essence, only ensure that you as the perceiver believe that you are a physical body. That's the only influence! It solidifies your belief, even when you play such an abstract game like chess, where physicality and space are of no importance at all! Still, by using pieces, and by using a board, and moving pieces in space, you solidify the belief of being a physical entity.

Now imagine that this game of chess that you see in front of your inner eye is broadcasted, say, via the internet to a thousand spectators. They are observing what is going on, and as soon as a piece moves on the board the feeling realities of all spectators change, instantly. It is just one piece of information that changes: where is a certain piece located now? And yet the impact is that all perceivers are immediately influenced by it. Their feeling realities change.

Now, let me summarize all of this. Ousia and perception bring forth all the potential experiences within the second round of creation. All the potential experiences within the second round of creation. It then depends on the core beliefs a perceiver has, how certain ousia are perceived. And of course it depends on the personal history of a perceiver, how a perception of ousia is internally transformed into a feeling reality. Thus, there is no such thing as an objective truth.

The details are always trumped by the feelings, and the feelings change continually. So, in a way, we have just discussed away space and physicality out of your experience. It's a bit weird, isn't it? It's a paradox, for you are still in your body and you want to stay embodied, as an embodied human being.

So, what do you do with this understanding? Well, don't fight your insights! At the same time, don't fight the core beliefs that allow you to share experiences in physical reality. That's the paradox! That means living the paradox. Not getting in conflict with this understanding of true reality, of light world, of ousia and perception – but maintaining a stable human facade at least, and a stable human consciousness without going crazy in these beliefs.

I tell you what: the more you open up to this, the weirder all of this gets. So, you need to be very stable, and willing to stay here in the physical. Otherwise, the surreal might overwhelm you. That is why we spend so much time with cultivating the awareness. We have spent so much time with cultivating your awareness to make you stable, so you are not the punching bag of the sentiments. Or like a ball in a pinball machine that is shot all around between the various ousia, not knowing who or what you are.

To make that even clearer, I want you now to open up to your temple in borderland. It's a shift in perspective, nothing more. And as you go there, well, go as a point of awareness – do not go there as a light body or as a kind of human. Go there without being contained in a vessel, but be a point of awareness. And as we have learned, a point, well, is actually really nothing, other than it does somehow exist.

Now, in the preparation for this segment, while cultivating your awareness, you were asked to become space, to become aware of the space around you and to feel as space. And now I ask you to feel as consciousness. Open up and *be* consciousness itself. Be the container; be the sky that contains all the clouds. At the same time, maintain the awareness of this point of consciousness that is in your temple in borderland. Now you are both. You are all of consciousness, containing all the ousia, all of light world. And you are a point of awareness that can perceive the ousia from a specific perspective.

Now imagine light world. And again, we have all these problems with the words for if we say "imagine light world as a vast firmament," then we are back in space. Okay, so be it, we have to communicate somehow. So, you might imagine it as a vast, vast firmament. All the ousia are like tiny dots; so many of them! So many ousia out there... and they are all within you. Yet you can see them from a specific perspective.

Now, find the ousia on the firmament that corresponds to the room your physical body is sitting in right now. Then, *be* there. I won't say *move* there, just *be* there and see this physical room from a bird's eye perspective. See the objects in the room as ousia, as light objects. Feel, or better said, sense the sentiments emanating from them, like from the chair you are sitting in right now. It might be your favorite chair; it's inviting and cozy. There might be a desk in your room; sense the desk. It might smell like work; work that you might like or not like. Roam around in your room. There might be some pictures on the walls that mean something to you.

These are all ousia that you placed there, and you charged them with sentiments. They ground you in your personal history. They remind you of who you are. Every moment, they stimulate a certain feeling reality within you, and you identify with it. As you move around in your room as a point of awareness, realize that it is absolutely in your power *not* to be influenced by the sentiments. You can sense them, but there is no need for you to transform them into felt feelings. That is the second benefit of lucid perception.

Lucid perception means being aware of all and at the same time being aware from a specific perspective. The first benefit is that the ego illusion ceases. It goes out the window, for you no longer identify with anything. The second benefit is that you become aware of the sentiments which want to pull you in, and you are capable of saying; "No! No more! No more! *I am the master of my feelings*. No object, be it my object, or anybody else's object, has the power to influence me, unless I allow it."

That's why I brought in light world. It's not the new playground for you to create the most amazing things, for they do not exist in separation. I brought light world in for you to understand the mechanics of the dream world of separation and to enable you to stay within separation without falling prey to it.

As a matter of fact, coming back for a moment to the game of chess, when the rules of chess were defined, *all* potential games sprang into existence, implicitly! They were just there! And each played game just enacts one of those already existing games. So, you cannot create a new chess game, it's impossible. You can just play an already existing game for the first time.

And the very same holds for separation! You could say separation is a game with exactly one rule: you express only with building blocks which are made out of separation. Boom! Here you have all the potential experiences within separation. I call it an ocean of oceans of scene spheres. It is vast, vast, vast... and it already exists! You just traverse through the scene spheres and experience them as a thread of time, but you do not create anything new! There is no true creation in separation.

Now, have a look at the compound ousia that composes your human body. It consists of physical components and non-physical components. You might typically picture the non-physical components somehow around your physical body, like your emotional body. If you consider memories, where are they? They need to be somewhere, so we'll place them close to your physical body, because you think they are connected to it.

But now let's go surreal. What if you strip away space as we have just done with the game of chess? What if the various components of your physical body are not even connected as you believe them to be? Your body is just a compound of ousia – but these ousia have no fixed position in space.

So, the fact that your arms are connected to your torso, well, is a matter of perception! You could be spread out all over light world. Actually, you are; same for your memories, and your emotional body. It is you who keeps it all together by the power of belief. Add some space to it, and you are able to arrange the ousia in a spatial way. Then the illusion becomes even more real. If you then identify with this physical body located in space, then you suddenly believe you are a body.

Well, not really, for seen from our current perspective, you may recognize how difficult it is to maintain that belief. As consciousness, it is very difficult to believe you are physical! That's why we had to take these drastic measures. We had to hypnotize you into believing yourself to be a physical body, for it is so unnatural... but it worked.

So, at some point you came to the belief that you are this physical entity consisting of two arms, two legs, a nose, and whatnot.

Yet, in reality, you are consciousness! You are All-That-Is, perceiving your content from a specific perspective. And the only thing that happened is that because of perception, you have identified with one ousia – you suddenly believed, "This is me."

With this identification came the fear of death. But as it was said in the intro song, "Always look at the bright side of death." There is no death. It's the death of an illusion, and you cannot call that a death. It's a freeing! It's a liberation! It's a coming back to the natural state. This understanding is true wisdom that needs to be applied.

The fundamentals of consciousness are very, very easy to understand. It is by applying the same fundamental principles to themselves, over and over again – like in a fractal, or in a deep recursion – that you get all these super complex environments. But then, no, no, no... it is *not* about you unraveling or undoing these structures, no! It is about dropping the belief that they are real, and then you are out – and be it only for a moment.

Be it only for a moment – a moment of enlightenment, a moment of embodied ascension.

241

A question comes up: if there are multiple entities, do all of these entities have a full replication of light world within them? And if so, how are the ousia and these light worlds synchronized? Otherwise, the entities couldn't have shared experiences.

Again, the question already relies on the notion of space, for the moment the term "entity" is used a "vessel" is usually implied, some kind of vessel. And if there is a vessel, then something has to be *in* that vessel.

But I contend that for a human it is very difficult to let that go. Therefore, I came up with the metaphor of a holomovie that plays within all entities. It's a good enough metaphor. You all know what a hologram is. It's a kind of photograph. You can split it in parts and all the information is kept in every part. Now, when you animate this, you have a holomovie. So, the same holomovie plays in all the entities. This is something the human can kind of easily accept. It's a little out there, but in a still acceptable way.

Today, I want to present a different metaphor which is simpler, and, I would say, more accurate, but very challenging: I say that there is just one light world, but there are many, many points of awareness that perceive light world, and these points actually have no extension – they are not vessels.

Feel into that. It's a bit uncomfortable, but it makes things so, so easy.

*

No matter which metaphor you prefer, if you prefer the metaphor of the holomovie that's played within each entity and perceived by each entity, or the metaphor of the points of awareness, the crucial point is:

*It is **one** dream of separation. It is **one** pondering of separation.*

That's why I say, "All is within."

That's why I say, "You are All-That-Is!"

The funny thing is that it seems like I am talking of a dream, but it's quite the contrary. You are living in a dream, and I speak of true reality. Can you imagine true reality to be true?

Speaking of "imagine," if you have read "The Lucid Dreamer," you might recall that I used the song "Imagine" as an example of an ousia that is highly charged with sentiments from people all over the world. And of course the idea came up to play "Imagine" as the entry music today. But as John Lennon was killed more or less to the day forty years ago, we felt, that this would not be a good choice. John Lennon and this song were played all over the media in the last week, and all the pity and mass consciousness became so strong that we decided not to play it as intro music. But we'll have it as the "extro." We're going to play it now, but I'd like to rephrase the lyrics a little bit as follows:

You might say I'm a lucid dreamer
But I'm not the only one
I hope someday you'll join us
And separation will be as one

I am Althar the Crystal Dragon. I've always been on the bright side of life, and I visit you on the light side of life. I hope to see you there as often as possible! And now, please, enjoy John Lennon once again. Good bye and see you next week.

(*Song plays*)

*

Joachim: Welcome back after an intense session. Oh, it was long!

So feel free to share or ask anything if there is anything to share or ask.

Participant 1: Yes, a very quick question. The ousia, it is in everything, also in those terrible, very sad memories, like the loved ones we lost, like my mother for example. She is there as a picture, here as well, in my head, everywhere, and all the things we did are all in me, so to speak... and when I see a picture or a photo of her, this picture I have... here, I think you can see it *(he shows the picture to the camera)*.

Joachim: Yes.

Participant 1: Well, it's all so meaningless! And this is very hard for me to... a part of me is just not ready... I don't know. It is ready, at the same time there is something really saying, "This is much too much."

At the same time, I'm seeing and feeling ousia in everything; in things which are very beautiful like playing the guitar or piano; listening to music. And also in the things which are very bothersome, or which you really would like to hate – like people chatting, noises, whatever – unfriendly people. And all this, these reactions, I perceive it and I get the ousia so to say, I feel it. There is all this ousia; many layered in a certain way, there are many layers. And if I feel it and see it, so to say, then I can let go of all these things which are bothering me, or which also are making me very happy. I'm free from this kind of distraction.

Is this ousia really also meaningless? Also if it's... well... it's meaningless... but it's... is it really like that? Also with our loved ones, because I get it, the example with teddy bear also, I get it...

Joachim: Yeah but, the statement is: you are the one who gives the meaning to it.

Participant 1: I know...

Joachim: And that's the point to understand. You are free to give the meaning to it, and then the more you identify with it, the closer you are, the more special is your relationship. And with that come, you might say, the good parts, but also the bad parts of a relationship. This is no judgment, it is just an observation. This is just how things work within separation. And I think it's pretty straightforward to see that.

It doesn't mean to reject anything – it doesn't mean that at all. It doesn't mean to reject the mother, but to see the broader picture. At the same time, be honest with yourself. Like, if you feel the grief and if she has not departed so long ago, then it's all still close, and if it was a close relationship, then that's just the way it is. Do not go in and fight it or try to convince yourself that this is meaningless. Not at all! The meaningless part means, well, this is just the way it is. You take color and you paint it on a white wall and you get a picture. That's all. What you paint is up to you, what you make of this is up to you, and that's how it works.

However, you could paint any kind of picture, and therefore each picture in a way is meaningless other than the meaning you yourself give to it.

This understanding is liberating! In a given situation with a personal relation, well, it might be difficult, but then again, think twice. Look at all the relationships you have, with whomever, and then look at all the problems you have, and you will track them down mostly to your relationships, because they are oh-so-special.

See, and the moment you realize that, you can ask yourself, "I can be in a relationship, but does it need to be a 'constantly sentiment triggering' relationship? Or can it be a free relationship – eye to eye, joined in suchness, open?"

I agree, with a mother or a loved one, this is not easy, and nobody says it is. But this doesn't change the fact of how these things work. It's like with gravity; if your mother falls out a window… well, gravity is just gravity, it's not bad or good, it's just the way it is.

The liberating understanding here is to see the mechanism, to be aware of it, and to allow this understanding to grow within you and not to get cold hearted or to get reclusive, no. You realize this, and because of this, you can act compassionately with everyone – for the sentiments that they are emanating, well, they are meaningless. What is meaningful is the consciousness behind it, which is beyond separation, but still believes itself to be encapsulated in some, whatever – a vessel or ousia. But you see the whole story, and therefore you can act completely different... as opposed to being in your own vessel with your own thoughts about yourself, clashing with everybody because they don't agree with you.

Participant 1: Okay, thank you very, very much.

Joachim: You're welcome.

Okay, then this was it for today. If I'm not mistaken, Christmas comes in ten days, so I will see you before Christmas, yes.

Let's have a wonderful wave for the photo. See you next week!

9. Bringing In the Christ Consciousness

Hello Everybody! Good to see you again! Another week has passed, and we are close to Christmas now, and maybe this becomes the topic of today. Actually, one of the topics is *bringing in the Christ consciousness*.

We start right away, as always, with cultivating the awareness. To do so, take on the position of a master, the posture of a master. Stretch your backbone, press your head against the sky, pull the chin in a little bit, let the shoulders fall backward, and relax all the rest of your body.

Create the cosmic mudra by placing the left hand into your right, the thumbs are horizontal, and you place your hands in your lap so that the small fingers touch your belly.

Close your eyes three quarters, and just breathe in and out through the nose; the mouth is closed. The tip of your tongue is touching the roof of your mouth and the backside of your teeth.

As always, I emphasize that cultivating the awareness is a non-doing. It's coming back to the natural state. It's not a struggle. It's not a fight with yourself, your feelings, or your emotions – it's just coming back to the natural state, by stopping doing, by becoming aware of your body; by becoming aware of the content of your mind, and not reacting to it anymore.

So, breathe in calmly through your nose. And even when I say "calmly," well, the breath is automatically calming down. It's not that you are doing anything with your breath; you just become aware of it.

As you breathe become aware how your belly moves slowly in and out.

Now I want you to become aware of your feet, specifically of the bones of your feet. It sounds a bit weird, but just place your awareness there, right inside the bones of your feet, of both feet simultaneously.

Now include the bones of your lower legs.

Include the bones of your knees... the bones of your upper legs...

It is very interesting to be aware of your bones, for usually you never notice them unless they are aching. Whenever you are asked to feel into your arm or your finger, you feel most often the skin, the sensations on the skin, but the bones, well, they are somehow hidden. They seem not to be alive. Yet, they provide your physical body stability. They carry you through your life, and of course there is lots of activity inside the bones, in the marrow – lots of activity. The marrow, in a way, is like a treasure chest. It's hidden within your body; you never think of it unless you are ill, but otherwise, you never notice it. But you can become aware of it; you can sense it.

Now become aware of your backbone... your complete backbone... it's a complex construct.

Include the bones of your hand, of both of your hands and your fingers.

Now include the bones of your arms... of your shoulders... and of your chest.

Finally, include your skull.

Now picture the whole skeleton of yours as it sits in the chair. Just the skeleton; strip away the flesh and the blood and the tissue and everything else – picture just the skeleton. You've seen skeletons often in all kinds of movies or in reality. Your skeleton is a major part of you. If you were to die and your body was to be put aside, well, this is what remains.

Actually, when new disciples wanted to join the community of the Buddha in the early days, the first task they had was to live for three months on a cemetery – a cemetery where the poor ones brought their dead people. These people didn't have any money to pay for a fire, so the bodies of their deceased were disposed at these cemeteries, and left to rot away. It was the task of the young disciples to tune into that, to see the decay of everything, for even though they were still alive, death was always around the corner. And that was what happened to a decaying body – in the end, it was just a skeleton.

This wasn't morbid in any way. It was just a way of pointing out how things truly are. And you can become aware of your skeleton in the same way. There is no death wish behind it, you simply see the skeleton as it is. While you live, it is so essential, and even when you die, it doesn't seem to change too much, although it's then absolutely devoid of life. Something has gone – the consciousness that made it alive has gone.

Again, feel right into your bones, into the bone marrow; the large bones, they have the bone marrow inside.

As you do, you can feel how you get really intimate with your physical body.

Now, while being aware of the totality of your skeleton, add the awareness of all of your flesh and inner organs.

It's a bit shocking isn't it? It's like a universe in itself. But where are *you* in this universe?

Good, now let go of these images and of this full body awareness, and change to pure observation. Just be aware of what happens. As you do, you might expand your awareness beyond your physical body. Just be aware of what is going on all around you.

When you catch yourself drifting away into your daydreams, thoughts, or memories – just come back to your body, stretch your backbone, pull in the chin a little bit. Assume a position of clarity, and then go back to observation.

You might say this is the way of the dragon. The dragon is not affected by any outer stimulus. The dragon notices the stimuli, but does not bow to them.

We are nearing the end of our ten week program, so I take this opportunity to emphasize again the importance of this very simple non-practice. It means to become the master in your own house, in your physical temple. It allows you to really become an embodied master; a master of your thoughts, feelings, and emotions.

Actually, you can do this throughout the whole day. Of course, it's advisable to cultivate your awareness once in a while, maybe daily, in a safe environment like we are in right now, where you are not disturbed. But of course there is no separation between this safe environment and your daily life. You can be in total awareness whatever you do! And when you are, then things usually get much easier, smoother; more enjoyable. Why? Because you leave out the false identities! You remain the master in the present situation.

If someone comes along and triggers you, you realize quickly what happened, and you can let go, if you so choose. That's the fruit of this non-practice. It makes your life so easy.

Now, let's come back to the sounds that are emanating from your Hara, your chest, your crown, and the spot above your crown. Become aware of them simultaneously as they radiate their sound. It's like a choir. And you can also feel this combined sound in your skeleton, in your flesh; it has a resonance – this is the sound of you.

Good... we'll play some music, and see who will join us today.

*

(*Music plays*: "The Long and Winding Road",
The Beatles)

Lyrics of the song:

The long and winding road
That leads to your door
Will never disappear
I've seen that road before
It always leads me here
Lead me to you door

The wild and windy night
That the rain washed away
Has left a pool of tears
Crying for the day
Why leave me standing here?
Let me know the way

Many times I've been alone
And many times I've cried
Anyway, you'll never know
The many ways I've tried

And still they lead me back
To the long winding road
You left me standing here
A long, long time ago
Don't leave me waiting here
Lead me to your door

But still they lead me back
To the long winding road
You left me standing here
A long, long time ago
Don't keep me waiting here
Lead me to your door

Yeah, yeah, yeah, yeah

*

I am Aouwa, a true self in expression.

What an honor it is for me to be with you today, just a few days ahead of Christmas.

Actually, we had a bit of a discussion amongst us. Who would come in today to present this session? We decided just a few moments ago it would be me, because today I'm going to speak as a true self to your true self.

Right now, you might be here, feeling yourself as a human façade; the human aspect of your true self. But you are also your true self, for the veil is thinning as the belief in separation is thinning. Actually, there was never a separation between you and your true self, just as there was never a separation between your true self and pure consciousness. It's all just a symptom of the illusion of separation.

So, you are here as your true self just as you are here as the morsel of incarnated human consciousness that attempts to go beyond separation on behalf of its true self.

Today's topic is *bringing in the Christ consciousness*. But before I can come to this topic, we have to once again repeat why this was necessary in the first place. Of course, the reason was the discovery of the standstill. To underline this most important insight and wisdom, we are going to have a long walk today – long walk along the long and winding road that you took through the world of separation.

Before we can start out, I ask you to join me. Join me as a point of awareness from where you can see Earth as floating in space. Just come to me; it's a shift in perspective. A shift in perspective and we see Earth, the blue planet, as it's spinning quietly. It looks so peaceful from out here.

Now, let's zoom out, go further away from Earth. As we do, we can see the sun, the huge sun of your solar system. We can see all the other planets. As you zoom out more and more and expand your awareness, you suddenly see the whole galaxy that your solar system is in – the Milky Way!

We continue moving in one direction, and suddenly there is not just one galaxy, there are many galaxies. Each galaxy looks like a tiny dot – so many, so many of them. And they also build structures, fogs, huge spirals.

And still we zoom out, and zoom out, and zoom out till the edge of your physical reality, wherever that is, and we just go beyond that as well. It's again a shift in perspective. As we do, we can realize that there are many, many universes. Each of them looks just like a bubble – huge inside, but in our expanded state, well, it's kind of tiny. And we go further beyond and further beyond, until we arrive in what you might call borderland, what Althar calls borderland.

Now, imagine all these physical universes as contained in a single bubble, floating in pure consciousness just like Earth floating in space. The inside of that bubble is huge – it is vast – yet, it represents just the physical aspects and the spatial aspects of separation.

One might ask, is this image real? Well, not really, for of course there is no space in pure consciousness. But it is real enough to give you an understanding of what separation is. It is real enough for us to have a basis for communication, to have a common image – which is always so important in communication.

Now, let's replace this representation of the physical aspects of separation with separation itself. We have often talked about scene spheres. A scene sphere is the sum total of all perceptions, feelings and thoughts that an entity has in a given moment. We might also say, it's a snapshot of its feeling reality in a given moment.

If you think in human terms, you might picture such a scene sphere actually as a sphere, because humans feel like living in a sphere. Everything around you is in a way "round"; the horizon is round, the sky above you. You are living in a sphere, so let's picture a scene sphere as a sphere.

Now, from our perspective, have a look at all the scene spheres you have lived through today. There are billions and billions of them – and these are just those that you have experienced! Today, you had many, many choices. When you woke up, you could have chosen to step out of your bed with your left or your right foot, to drink coffee or tea, to eat this or that. There were so many potential choices, but just one scene sphere per moment was experienced. However, all the other scene spheres already existed. You could have chosen them! You could have experienced them.

So, the amount of scene spheres is vast. It's gigantic. That's why I speak of an ocean of oceans of scene spheres. What does that mean? Well, you know what an ocean is. Imagine each drop of this ocean was also an ocean. And actually we would need a different term, we would need to say "an ocean of oceans of oceans of oceans of oceans of scene spheres." These are all the potentials that separation holds.

These scene spheres represent everything that ever was experienced, is experienced, and will ever be experienced.

Just like with the game of chess – when the rules were made, all games were instantly there, implicitly. They did not need any representation. And the very same holds for separation! A thought of separation – BOOM – all the scene spheres are there.

258

Now, picture them from our vantage point. Picture this ocean of oceans. Picture it as also being contained in a sphere – it's gigantic.

This is the eternal now moment.

It is vast! No brain and especially no linear brain could ever fathom this.

There's a reason why we always have to break everything down into a linear mode, linear words, linear thinking, linear images, and today we will do exactly the same. We have to do this, because otherwise we couldn't communicate. Of course, there are non-linear ways to experience and to describe what we'll be talking about, but as you are biased by your human consciousness towards linearity, we are going the linear way.

Let's first consider where this eternal now moment of separation came from. Therefore, consider God-consciousness, the oneness, beingness. At one point, this God-consciousness might have pondered, "Well, it would be great if I could share my experience with some others, with equals, so that I'm in the joy of sharing. But how could I do that? How could that be possible? If I wanted to do that, I would need to cut a bit out of myself. I would need to separate something from me, so that there are others that are like me."

And as this thought occurred, a monumental reflection came about: the ocean of oceans of scene spheres – *that* is the reflection of the thought of separation. And even before this God-consciousness could understand the impossibility of its thought, it became curious and entered into this vast ocean. Figuratively speaking, it entered at the edge of the ocean into several of these scene spheres. And suddenly, God-consciousness, or parts of it, were *in* separation, not as one – *but as many!*

Then the journey began. And this is where we will begin our journey today, for that was actually the starting point of the journey of the true selves.

Did it really happen that way?

Nobody knows, and nobody can know. But according to me, and according to others, this is a story that fits our experiences quite well, quite nicely. It also fits the linear mind – which might be proof that it didn't occur that way – but for our undertaking, it is good enough! Why? Because the actual question is not so much, "How did this all come about?" But, "What is the way out? *What is the way out of separation?*"

So, what we are doing today is taking a walk along the long and winding road that the true selves took through the worlds of separation. And for this, we have set up a theme park. Along our path there are stages left and right where holo-movies play. They are radiating out sentiments, so you can easily feel and relive what happened back then. And I really want you to relive that to the best of your abilities. This is a fast forward through separation. There's a very important reason why I want us to have this journey today. You will see it at the end or maybe in the middle of our trip.

So, we start with the first holomovie stage.

Actually, there's nothing.

Still, I start the music even though there is not yet anything. I will accompany our journey with some music, so that you can go into feeling mode more easily.

(Music plays)

Imagine how that might be... You enter the worlds of separation. You come from God-consciousness and you enter, figuratively speaking, at the edge of this vast, vast ocean where there is not yet much to experience. So, you find yourself in a sphere which is more or less empty.

On the stage you see here, there is not too much to see at first – just something like a kind of question mark. A real question mark would be too much, because you don't know any symbols yet. You don't know who you are. You don't know where you came from. You don't know what you could do. Such was the first experience of the true selves entering separation.

Then suddenly, something changed drastically, but you had no idea what it was. Not the slightest idea. Because there was no time and no reference point whatsoever, we cannot even put a time tag on how long the nothing-state lasted, if it took, say, a second or twenty five eons. It cannot be said.

However, at some point there was an *intent*. It came up. Why? Well, that's the nature of consciousness. It can have intents, and it can be aware of itself. This holds even in separation. The only difference in separation is that all the intents and all the awareness are also based on separation.

So, the intent came up and you became aware of the reflection of it, from yourself, from the pure energy that you are also. That was the first change! Suddenly, there was *something!* It was not just you and nothingness, but *there was something,* and you started to play with intents. You explored your environment. What intents could you have? To this day, nobody really knows why an intent comes about. It's a creative impulse that's suddenly there. It's a mystery. It's the "creator capability."

So, you explored your intents and your reflections. Of course, sooner or later you identified with your reflections, because this gave you something to lean on. You repeated the same intent in order to get the same reflections. Thus, you had some stability in your beingness. Again, nobody can really say how long that took, but you played and played until at some point you felt something that wasn't quite like you. It was different. You knew this was not an intent that came from you, but a reflection from somewhere else. Still, you became aware of it.

This was when you met "another entity." And what a great joy that was... another entity! You were not alone in this vast void, this vastness, or whatever you might call it. There was another entity, and this entity also had intents. So, you both could act out together, explore together. Not only that – the other had intents that you never would have had! So it was enriching. Also, you could mirror yourself in the other! That was a totally new experience.

Then, of course, more entities came along and so groups were formed. The way entities formed groups back then is very similar to how human children form groups today. Of course, children form groups in the neighborhood where they were born. Here they find the potential members of their group.

Same here! Whenever someone was "close" to you – close in their energy, because there was no space – a bonding took place, specifically if, maybe by chance, you had the same original intents as the other entity. If you had created the same beliefs about yourself, then of course you would be attracted to each other. That is what group members are. They share the same beliefs – not to say the same illusions – about themselves. And by doing so, they solidify the beliefs they have about themselves.

That is how the spiritual families came into being. Entities sharing the same beliefs about their existence, about the environment – they came together. And as they did, as they repeated their intents over and over again, the blueprints were created. Because they were hanging on to the same intents and repetitions and feedback loops, the ousia underlying these intents were solidified so much that they became what are now called the blueprints. And once an ousia is the basis for a life being lived out, well, it's solidified over and over and over again. Of course, then it's hard to get over those blueprints, right?

So, the true selves continued with their experiences. Nobody knew where he came from, but there was so much to discover in these worlds of separation – even though up to this point nobody had the notion of "separation." It was just about discovering oneself, discovering the reflections one could create.

Of course, there was a lot of exchange; not only in the positive, but also in the negative. Frictions came up and the first false identities. Everything that false identities stimulate in a human was stimulated here also. There were likes and dislikes; other groups and other families that you met, with totally different belief systems, well, they were considered to be some kind of "enemy." Sometimes it was interesting to exchange, and it happened. But other families were so alien to you that fights broke out; wars broke out in the non-physical.

Can you imagine a war in the non-physical? Without having a physical body, where nothing you do has a real consequence? Well, you tried other things than humans do in a war. You tried to trap entities in some mirror cabinet, something like that, but it is not that they felt real pain like you know as a human. So, all the fighting was very fast, very intense, and instantaneous. This went on for eons, and eons, and eons. Nobody can say how long it really was. However, at some point, the first entities realized, "Wait a minute! We are always doing the same things. We are repeating our storylines, our plots, and our experiences. Yes, we might change our vessels, we might change our belief systems even without knowing, but in the end, it's always the same plots being acted out."

There was a group called Uru which you might describe as "The Master Scientists," or as a mixture of mystics and engineers – that might be the best description for them. They realized very soon, "Hold on, something isn't quite right here!" They did not go as deep into separation as others did. They did not pile up so many beliefs. Instead, they started trying to research the mechanics of separation. Oh, initially they didn't have the term "separation," but at some point, it was Uru who came up with this concept, with this way of describing what really happened.

The members of Uru realized that there is something one might call "going within." They researched what it meant to react to reflections. And that was a major breakthrough. They experimented with explicitly changing what we are now calling core beliefs. They did so by compressing themselves, by exposing themselves to a compression so that they had to take on new beliefs. And as they did, they realized that their whole life experience changed! Very interesting!

At the same time, they realized that there was no way to ever come out of this weird world by applying this kind of compression and taking on new beliefs. Quite the contrary! You needed to let go of them! That was their assumption! Letting go of all beliefs will be the way out!

So they researched in this direction and continued with their compression experiments. They realized, yeah, they can compress each other, and have very new life experiences. But even in these new life experiences, they came again to the conclusion that they were just repeating the same story lines. At that point, they started again to let go of the beliefs that were compressed into them. But when they finally managed to let them go, they were back where they came from. It was not a *final* letting go. It didn't go all the way to the core. So, that's what Uru has been doing for a long, long time.

As the true selves continued with all their experiences, more and more and more of them were realizing that separation really has just one taste, which is the taste of repetition.

Put yourself into such an entity a we come to the next stage in our theme park. Here you see a holomovie that shows a true self that has recognized the eternal repetition, but knows no way out. An entity who has been around for eons, who has fought in many, many wars, who has had all kinds of relationships, and then realized, "It is all just repetition! Again and again and again!" The entity collapsed! It was stopping any outer activity, but not in the sense of going within to see what is there. No! It closed the doors and replayed the same movies over and over again – it hung on to its memories and fears. It collapsed. It was like a black hole: nothing came out of it anymore. And as others saw that, as ever more entities also realized what it meant to be trapped in separation, in always the same activities, they said, "We need to do something!"

This was called the standstill. Standstill does not mean that everything stops moving. *The standstill is the understanding that nothing really changes!* In the depth, there is no change. On the surface, there is constant change. But everything else, the experiences as such, they are essentially always, always the same.

For a human, this sounds a bit weird, outlandish. For obviously, if you look at this ocean of oceans of scene spheres from the perspective of a human life span, then of course you can only have so many experiences in your life and then you say, "What's the point? There's still so much out there to experience."

But imagine you had to go to your job every morning; do whatever you do, like, take some form and fill it out, work with a client, or whatever it is. Imagine you will not only do it until you retire in some decades or years, no, no. You do it eon, after eon, after eon, after eon. If that were to dawn on you, well you might get a bit of an anxious feeling and say, "Maybe I should try to get out of this; otherwise I might just go nuts."

In other words, they came to the understanding that *the standstill is everywhere! It is everywhere in separation.* This is the number one topic I want to underline today, and I underline it three hundred thousand times! *Never forget about this!* Do *not* try to become the super master in separation. You did that for eons. *It is not about replicating God-consciousness within separation.* It just doesn't work. It's futile. *The standstill is everywhere in separation, and you can feel it.*

So, this knowingness spread amongst the true selves, amongst the spiritual families, and a big gathering was held. In the gathering, everyone was complaining and we thought about the different things we could do. One plan was brought forth by the group of Uru. On the stage to my right, you see this act as a holomovie. You might have been in that gathering. It was one of the major milestones of separation and of the experiences in separation.

So, Uru stood up, and they explained what they had done with their research. They spoke about the compression, and the principle of letting go, and of going within. They also said that they did that themselves, and came very close to the final letting go. They denoted this "coming very close" as the principle of ascension. It was near real, but not really real. They knew that it was real "in principle," but still there remained some doubt within them.

That's why they brought forth the idea of replicating their approach on a much grander scale in something that was meanwhile discovered, physical reality. They said, "If we can compress morsels of consciousness into physicality so that they believe themselves to be of physicality existing in this ultra slow motion realm, in this utmost compression of consciousness, then there is a chance that when these entities finally come to the conclusion that there is a standstill, an everlasting repetition, and they start letting go, that they really let go of everything, because there is no other way left that could be tried." That was the hope. And Uru also said, "We need to be very sure that this works. Compression alone, as we have noticed, does not suffice. We also need a hypnosis, which is nothing other than a very deep implanted core belief that might be called 'I am of matter', or 'I am a physical body'."

So it was agreed to follow this plan. Many, many families and true selves took part in this joint venture. Thus, Earth was selected, and it was prepared. It took a long time. The biological life forms came into existence; it took a long time. Then, at some point, the time was right to send the first morsels of consciousness of the true selves down there. Here on the stage to my left, you can see this scene. There are a number of true selves, or better said emanations of true selves, gathered. They knew that they would go through a huge compression and hypnosis.

Their true selves did not know if this would work out or not. They could be crippled for the rest of eternity. So they promised something, they made a big vow to each other. This vow went like this: *whoever comes first, whoever makes it to the other side comes back and helps the others.*

Then they went into the compression chamber, which I explained elsewhere as applying a series of reverse atomic explosions, for you have to understand that the energies on the physical plane are rough. If you tear apart a few atoms, you get an atomic explosion. Now, if you want to act on that stage, you have to do the reverse! You compress yourself with the same force. And that was not very pleasant and left a number of traumas. Well, that's the way it was. However, you were not directly squeezed into a biological life form, not at all, because you were still too light after the compression.

You started your journey around planet Earth as ethereal bodies. You bonded with some biological life forms, and slowly glided into them. You looked through their eyes, felt how it was to be like them without really being them. It's like riding a horse. You sit on the back of the horse, well, you are not a horse, but you can feel kind of similar. Then you progress and project yourself into the body and watch or see through the eyes of the horse. Well, then it's much more real, but still not really real, because you know you can get out at any time.

However, as you did this, at some point you were caught in the process of biological birthing, and that was when the hypnosis really struck. You were in that egg... and the sperm came... and when both came together, then the hypnosis struck and you bonded specifically to the atoms of the DNA of the fertilized egg. You believed on that level of yourself, "I myself am matter!" As the egg with its DNA divided itself into more and more cells to build the body, well, so did you. And suddenly you were woven into this physical entity.

We from the other side, we cheered! We cheered, for consciousness and matter have bonded. And this is something that couldn't be anticipated. It wasn't clear that it was possible at all, for consciousness and matter are like fire and water. But it worked out! Yes, by means of hypnosis, and compression, and for a high, high price, for now the entities were totally on their own once again. They had no recollection of where they came from, their true selves or their common story. Not even of the standstill! In a way, they started out just like we did as true selves entering the first empty spheres of separation.

It didn't take too long until the first amongst them understood the principle of separation and the principle of repetition. However, this was very rare; there were only a few. In the meantime, the first cultures arose; Lemuria, Atlantis. Atlantis specifically made great, great progress in science, because they were not burdened by weird beliefs of a punishing God. Just out of curiosity, they played with consciousness, played with energies, played with crystals. And yes, we had the first ascensions back then. So we knew it would work.

271

But mass consciousness can only be stretched so much, and then, in a way, it snaps back. And so it did in Atlantis. Atlantis fell, and to this day, it is the archetype of a culture that tumbled. The implications were huge for everybody involved. The power games that were played were awful. It left big, big marks on all the souls of those who were incarnated. And that was a time when so many vows of "never again" were made. "Never again will I approach technology, for see what happens! Never again will I try to convince others to incarnate, if this is what happens. Never again will I approach enlightenment!" For enlightenment was also one of the endeavors. Going within, they started going within in groups. They came very far because mass consciousness was still very thin, it wasn't too difficult back then.

Let's continue our walk. Atlantis fell. But of course, the story continued. It took a while, you went underground; fresh ones came in – fresh ones who didn't carry the burden of the fall of Atlantis. At some point you came up from the ground, and new cultures were built, like Egypt.

Egypt was very interesting, because in Egypt you replicated some of the insights you'd learned in Atlantis. We had great mystery schools in Egypt. You literally acted out scenes to confront the adepts with their greatest fears, so they were prepared when they faced the beyond. That was deep. And of course the greatest mystery and the greatest fear of all living entities, of humans specifically, is the fear of death. In Egypt, you had ways to simulate that, to go beyond death, to make sure that the human understood there is no such thing as death.

However, we on the other side felt that it took way too long. And of course the Egyptians also started playing the old games again, this priesthood against that priesthood and all the rest of that, as always. So, we felt an example would be needed. An example would be needed to highlight for everyone what it means to be ascended, enlightened. This was the idea of collectively bringing in the Christ consciousness. And so it was decided to do just that.

This could not be done easily. It also required a long preparation. The entity that was appointed to come in for that role had to be prepared; the parents had to be prepared for the high energies. The community, even the disciples had to be prepared for this occurrence.

When this finally took place, the eve of Christmas that you have in a few days, it was a brilliant, brilliant milestone in our common journey through separation.

It was known that bringing in the Christ energy through a living entity would not result in, say, an infection of enlightenment that spreads immediately throughout all the humans. No, it was meant as a standard; as a light post to show it is possible, to demonstrate it is possible.

What is Christ? What does it mean to bring in the Christ consciousness? It means to bring in the knowingness of "I am that I am"; the knowing-ness of "All is within. I am the living light, no matter what. I am not dependent on separation. Well, my body may be, but that which I am is *not*!" That is what bringing in the Christ consciousness means, and that is what we have assisted with on the other side. Feel into that, into what it means... bringing in the Christ consciousness to set an example.

So, Yeshua came in. He didn't live too long, he didn't teach too long. He could have easily bypassed or escaped the crucifixion, but there was a reason not to do that. *The reason was to demonstrate to the world, and even to the future world, that there is no need to fear death*. He did not escape. He took his cross, so to speak, and he died on the cross, but did he die? No, *he demonstrated that death is an illusion!* He ascended! And those who had eyes to see, they saw him afterwards. That was the sign post. That was the example. We made it, you made it; we were all a part of it one way or the other.

Now, you know what happened from there. Some took the messages of Yeshua to heart, but many did not. They formed churches, and again the power plays began, as always, but at least there was the knowingness, and there were witnesses that it is possible.

So, you joined the churches. You created them, and you left them, or you were thrown out. You continued with mystery schools in Europe. "The many ways you've tried"; those were the lyrics of the song. "The many ways you've tried."

Then came World War II, and when the atomic weapons were finally thrown and exploded, it was a bit like in Atlantis. There was a great, great fear on the other side that this whole experiment would just terminate. It had already taken a long time, and we had the first positive results. Of course, we also knew that there were many, many not so good results in terms of suffering, pain, and death.

When the atomic explosions occurred, it was clear that it was time for many who were not incarnated at the time to incarnate again. Those who were already advanced on their path decided to return to Earth, to do it together and, let's say, instill a second wave of bringing in the Christ consciousness. And of course, you have been amongst them.

Now, here we are, and our long and winding path actually splits. There is a path for each and every one of you that you will walk alone. I will continue my narration, but each of you is now on your own. Just walk alone; you'll find your way.

It's a bit foggy here, it's not so clear. Just keep walking.

As you look ahead, you might see or sense something in the distance, a kind of a figure. As you come closer, you realize, oh my God, this is the most important teacher I have ever had in my life. He is standing right here. You know who that is. So approach that teacher. You might have met him or her in this lifetime, or it might be a figure from a book. It might be a saint from the past, an ascended master. You know the most influential figure in your spiritual life; he or she or it is standing here, waiting for you; waiting to greet you.

So, approach your teacher, eye to eye, heart to heart. Join in suchness.

Feel the joy in your teacher, for there is nothing more beautiful for a teacher than seeing how the seed opens up. It might take a long time, but when it does, oh it's beautiful for the teacher. That's the greatest joy for the teacher. And if the student even goes beyond the abilities of the teacher, that's all the better.

Now, make a *Namaste* or a *Gassho* gesture to your teacher and move on, along your long and winding road.

You realize, oh, there is another one. Another teacher you had. And not just one; there are many! They are lined up, they are waiting for you. You know you didn't just have one teacher; you had many, many, many. Some stood out, but others, they were somehow in the background, you didn't really notice them. It might even be a teacher at school, someone who just said a phrase that touched you and who might not even notice, or so you thought. But here they are. Just walk along and greet them, each and every one – this long, long line of teachers and inspirers that you had not only in this lifetime, but in all of your lifetimes.

They've come to greet you. They've come because of what you are doing right now. They know of our common story. Take your time and greet them. Some of them you might not have seen for a long time. Some of them you might see or feel in this reality, in this realness, for the first time.

Good, now, continue your walk. And as you continue, you might realize that you know this environment, you have been here before. The road you have taken has led you directly to your temple in borderland.

So, enter your temple; the temple that is yours and yours only. You are welcome here. And as you enter the door coming from the direction of separation, you see the other door – the other door that leads straight into the Third Round of Creation. It's a long and winding road that led you here to this door, and it will never disappear; unless you totally let go of separation.

Now, open that door, but do not step out. This is the Third Round of Creation; true creation, undistorted creation. The knowingness of this is called the Christ consciousness. You can come here anytime, and you can go through that door whenever you choose; that will be the final letting go. It is unknown if you will be able to come back once you do the final letting go. The light body might be ready, you might be ready internally to come back as a conscious projection into the realms of separation, but in fact, this is unknown. This is something that you will have to decide when the time comes.

Recall the meeting that the true selves had. You were amongst them, vowing, "Whoever comes first assists the others." *Right now, I want you to let go of this vow!* For back then, when you made that vow, you didn't know what you were promising. It's time to let that go. *If you choose to go back, go back without any obligation. Go as a free being, as a sovereign being,* as someone who *knows;* as someone who is aware of his moments of enlightenment, of his moments of embodied ascension; as someone who knows of the ways of consciousness which, well, may once again trap him for a while – but it's getting easier and easier to go beyond that and free yourself again.

So, why not choose once again to bring in the Christ consciousness? It's brought in on a personal level. You cannot bring it in for anybody else, but you can inspire others. You can set the example just like Yeshua did. No need for you to get crucified though; that play has already been acted out.

I said you can come back here anytime, and if you want to go towards the Third Round of Creation, do so in a quiet moment. Today, I invite you to just come back. It's not a rush anyway. So, have the intent of having a light body, and feel the light body around your physical body.

What a journey! What a journey. *It is the understanding that separation is static; there's no true creation, no matter where you look and how long you look.* There's no way to replicate heaven in separation, it's impossible, and there's no need for it, because separation is just a dream. It's a thought that is actually already gone, for it is impossible in the first place.

Again, feel your skeleton. Ground yourself in your physical body. Feel your flesh, feel your bones, and feel your light body. Allow your physical body to mimic your light body.

Althar just handed me a sheet of paper which is titled "The Homework Challenge." It's saying that for the next session, which will be our last session, you have to bring either a glass of champagne or wine – no matter what time you have in your time zone when we have the meeting. It's always a good chance to have a glass of champagne or wine together when Christmas is just over and the New Year is right around the corner – and we will celebrate this ten week program. So, that's your challenge for the next week. I think that's not too hard. But don't drink the champagne before. That might be hard.

I am Aouwa. I am the beginning, the end, and the beyond of All-That-Is, and so are you. Thank you.

*

Joachim: I see that most are back. Some still have their eyes closed.

I think the homework is clear, right?

As always, if anybody has a remark, please feel free to say something or ask something.

Participant 1: Just amazing, thank you, thank you, thank you. And Merry Christmas!

Joachim: Yes, and same to you all! Merry Christ consciousness!

Participant 2: Merry Christ consciousness to all, and thank you.

I also have a question; just, this is wonderful, seeing all the teachers in our lives, leading up to the doorway that Aouwa was talking about. But when I try to integrate that with the final letting go, it seems to me that I've got to let go of all these teachers. And in your core books, it talks about letting go of everything – beliefs, passions, everything, all these ideas. I guess I'm seeing that as overwhelming, it's such a gigantic project, that final letting go, even though I can see it intellectually. There's a part of me I guess that's holding on to the teachers. Like Jesus – I grew up in a Jesus church, and I've done the "Course in Miracles" for many years, and it's part of me – readiness, Christ consciousness. Then it sounds like when I read the books, or hear... Althar said a few weeks ago we have to let go of trust... when I've been trusting in Jesus, or you, or Althar, or Joachim. Is letting go of trust letting go of everything? Do you want to speak to this; any of you beings want to speak to this final letting go?

Joachim: It is huge, it is really huge, and this is why Aouwa spoke about the principle of ascension. Like, well, you see it, you know it, but it's not yet real. You still cling to separation a little bit; there is something that wants you to stay in separation, to believe in the reality of separation once again.

The moment you truly understand there is no separation, then you will not be separated from what you have perceived as your teachers. Instead, you can join in suchness without the outer façade. But again, this is something that is really huge. It is *so* huge, and that is the reason why it is not done very often, and especially not done so often while one is still in a physical body. I like to say – and nobody likes to hear it – but I am convinced that the moment you die, you have a super great chance to really grasp the illusionary nature of separation, for then you are beyond your body and you know for real that things go on. And ideally, you have prepared yourself with cultivating your are awareness and your light body; so death is a tremendous chance.

The trick is to realize that there is no true death. If you still want to speak of death, then you have to see it as a birth. It's your own true birth. You birth yourself by letting go of the false assumption that you are a physical body. As you do, all these notions of trust and teachers and separation, and all the words that I just used, they go out the window. For in a moment of enlightenment, as all of you have experienced I assume, these questions are just irrelevant.

It's only when you bring in the memories of separation, and the wish to be special, or whatnot – to save something, to bargain with separation about your story – that is when the melancholy comes in, when the feeling of, say, sacrifice comes in. "Oh, I sacrifice my teachers if I let go." No, you honor them by following their example.

That is what Yeshua would ask of you. "Don't hang on to me, guy!"

That's the same as the saying, "When you meet Buddha on the road, kill him!"

Not in a literal way, but in a way of don't hang on to him! Don't be the eternal student. On the other hand, it's very, very difficult to not confuse yourself by pretending to be enlightened. Like, I pretend to myself that I'm realized. Yeah sure, everybody wants it. But it is really huge. It is really huge, so be content with moments of enlightenment, and go from there. Be honest with your feelings, and your feelings of appreciation of the teachers you had, and the fact that you don't want to let them go. Be honest about that. Still, open up. Open up again and again, and see with the Eye of Suchness. See things as they truly are.

The teachers are also just entities, running through all these scene spheres, and you've met each other which is great, but apart from that, there is no real difference between any of us. Our stories are different, but where we come from is identical, and where we go to, also. It doesn't mean that it's boring or that we are all the same. It just means, well, that's the way it is. It's about going beyond separation and finally experience true creation.

Ah, Aouwa is still here! *(chuckles)*

Participant 2: Thank you all of you for being here. Thank you all.

Participant 3: A teacher of mine refers to our teachers as "The Royal Entourage". I like that.

Joachim: Yes.

Participant 3: I give my gratitude to The Royal Entourage.

Joachim: Absolutely.

Participant 3: Sharing that to all.

Joachim: Yes... and it's a give and take, no? And it will not be so long until you stand there along this long and winding road, greeting some of your friends along the way that finally got what you said, and hey, here they are!

Participant 3: I have goose bumps!

Joachim: So, I think it's enough for today. Enjoy Christmas, enjoy your Christ consciousness, let it shine out, or let it shine just for yourself, as you like. But bring champagne next week, that's important!

So, see you next week! Oh, the waving... I need to find the right key. Where is it... here... another wave... wonderful!

Thank you! See you next week.

10. The Song of the Dragon

Welcome everybody! Welcome to this final session of our ten week program! I hope you all had a good Christmas, and you are bursting with Christ consciousness, so we can bring that in for our final session.

As always, we start out with cultivating the awareness. So, you know what to do. Take on the posture of royalty, the posture of the master, by straightening the backbone, by pressing the head against the sky and pulling the chin in a little bit.

Place your left hand in your right hand, the thumbs are horizontal and touch each other. Then place your hands in your lap so that your little fingers are touching your lower belly. The eyes are three quarters closed, the mouth is closed. You breathe in through the nose, and you breathe out through the nose.

Let the breath come and go without interfering in any way.

Now become aware of both of your feet.

Include your lower legs in your awareness, your knees, your upper legs, and your buttocks.

Now add the awareness of your hands, your lower arms, your belly, your upper arms, and your shoulders, your chest.

Notice how the body calms down, how the mind calms down.

Include your throat and your neck in your awareness.

Now include your entire head.

Extend your awareness for some twenty centimeters around your physical body. Be aware of what is going on close to your physical body. Simultaneously, keep the awareness of your physical body.

As you become aware of all of your body and the space around it, the notion of a center of your body somehow ceases.

As soon as you perceive anything, you typically assume to have a center. A center that might be somewhere in your head where your physical sense organs are located; or maybe around your heart area, or your belly – but in any case, you feel like you have a center. Somehow, as you open up your awareness, you can become aware of your perceptions without reverting to some center. Realize that holding on to a center greatly solidifies the illusion of separation. So, when you are capable of letting go the idea of having a center, it eases all your experiences in separation.

Now let go of all of your body awareness and just observe what is going on. Observe what phenomena arise on your inner screen, no matter where they come from, be it from your body, or from the outside, or other star systems. Just be aware. Once a phenomenon arises, you just observe it without associating it to anything; without chasing it or following it. Just witness what is going on without judging.

Once in a while, come back to your body posture. Stretch your backbone. Make sure your head is not falling to the side, or to the front. If you are sitting very straight, you do not need any muscle force, so you can sit very relaxed, without any tensions. Then you go back to pure observation.

We have spoken about light world and the ousia, formations in consciousness. They are the basis for any perception. We have discussed how each ousia is charged with sentiment, which is then perceived and converted into phenomena by the perceiver.

The sentiment can be seen as a kind of "vibration." You might also term it a "sound," even though you cannot hear it with your physical ears. Still, it's a resonance, a vibration that you can pick up. Your physical body consists of many, many ousia. It's a highly complex compound ousia, and it also emanates a certain vibration.

Right now, feel into your skeleton, into your bones.

How does it feel to be a human? How does it feel to have such a skeleton? You know how that feels, and to that feeling there corresponds a sentiment with a certain vibration. So, how does it feel to be physical? This is nothing you could do wrong; you cannot fail at it.

Also, there are many non-physical parts of your human body as well as all the wisdom that you have realized in this lifetime and also wisdom that you brought with you from previous lifetimes. All of these are also ousia, and they emanate a certain vibration. The same holds for anything you have ever experienced. There are many, many layers to this totality of sounds, of resonances, emanating from the body ousia that you are.

Right now, make it simple. Feel into yourself – how does it feel to be a human right now? How does it feel, in this very moment, to have lived your life?

You can distill it into a single sound.

It has many, many layers. It is rich, it has depth to it. This is *your* sound of being a human. This is the sound of your story as a human.

Even though this sound changes, there is also a certain stability to it; a constant. The wisdom that you have realized doesn't change too much. The physicality, the corporeality of you – well, that does change – but the feeling of being in the physical doesn't change too much.

It also contains a feeling that doesn't change at all: it is the feeling of *I exist.*

I exist! This also has a sound to it as you experience it here in separation.

So, feel all of this simultaneously: I exist, the corporeality of your physical body, your story, the wisdom you have realized.

This is the sound of you as a human.

Good. Let go of that sound and feeling for a moment and come back to pure observation.

*

So much can be conveyed in silence. That's beautiful. That's the beauty of being together in silence while still being joined.

So, we'll have some music, and Althar will join us.

*

(*Music plays*)

I am Althar, the Crystal Dragon.

Welcome to each and every one of you. Please, come and join in our meeting dimension. It is decorated like a ball room with some, well, not Christmas decorations, but Christ-consciousness decorations. We have a lot to do today and Christ-consciousness will play once again a major role.

Please arrange yourselves in a circle. Sit in a circle, because I want to take a round and greet you personally – from eye to eye and heart to heart.

We had a long ride through these ten weeks, not to say the last ten eons. Today, we are here for the finale of our ten week program and I want to congratulate you that you have been here, that you heard the call, and that you were brave enough to come.

As I make my round to greet you, you may feel other presences through me, for today I come in as many. With me here is Yeshua, and all the Christ-consciousness he ever had. With me is Shakyamuni, as well as a whole bunch of ascended masters – you might say the usual suspects.

They are with me today, for we are all in a certain way ambassadors of creation, and we can join in suchness. We do so today! Why? Because many of you have relations with a few of them, so they have come here today to assist you, to assist me, to assist us in celebrating a wonderful journey and in reaching a wonderful, well, not end point, but milestone on your road to embodied ascension.

So, let me finish my round.

Good.

Before we start with today's main topic, let me briefly summarize the three pillars of my messages. The number one is true wisdom. What is true wisdom? True wisdom allows you to go beyond separation. It comes from clarity. It comes from knowingness. It illuminates the illusions. It provides the means and the insights to appease your doubting mind, and finally to see things as they truly are. That is true wisdom. Also, true wisdom needs to be pragmatic. Thus, a sign of true wisdom is its simplicity. True wisdom is the first of the three main pillars of my messages.

Second, we have true compassion. Compassion first and foremost for you, for with the true wisdom, you have realized that going beyond separation is somewhat difficult. You don't just do it in the blink of an eye. No, it takes a while – not to say lifetimes, many lifetimes even. But the true compassion allows you to see this as it is without judging you for failure or for anything. More than anything, true compassion sees that separation has never really occurred the way you have thought it has occurred. Your story that you lived through in this lifetime and the previous lifetimes, this was just one path through the scene spheres of the ocean of oceans of scene spheres. You did not create any of these! You just experienced them. Therefore, you can, in a way, forgive yourself if you have the feeling that some things you did weren't that great. It was an experience that was already there.

That is the greatest compassion. Well, actually, the greatest compassion is forgiveness for you and also for everybody else, for everybody else is on the same route as you. Nothing that ever happened to you and nothing that you ever did happened in reality! These were just experienced potentials that were not created by you! That is true compassion. It allows you to overlook everything that you might otherwise see as a fault or failure or damage in yourself or others.

This is deep. At the same time, it is very simple. It's liberating.

The third pillar is, of course, true practice, because true wisdom and true compassion would be mere mental acrobatics if they were not applied in your real life. So, true practice is the cornerstone! Without it, well, all these discussions would be rather meaningless. It would be another book on the shelf, another wonderful idea, but for what?

True practice is in the domain of the human. This is what the human can and should do.

What true practices do we have?

First, of course, is choosing the Eye of Suchness. Whenever you feel you are once again caught in the dream of separation and you remember true reality, you choose the Eye of Suchness. You stop making the things that you perceive real.

You stop believing in their reality. That is utmost clarity. That is wielding the sword of clarity. Choosing the Eye of Suchness – a wonderful tool. It has to be applied!

Then, cultivating the awareness; becoming the master in your own house; becoming the master of your emotions, feelings, and thoughts. That in itself is liberating. That in itself allows you to act instead of constantly reacting, reacting to outer stimuli, to outer triggers or whatever comes in and pushes you around. You can say, "No more!" Not just as a thought, no, but as an action, as a letting go. You are no longer at the mercy of any outer stimulus. That is the fruit of cultivating your awareness.

Then, of course we have cultivating the light body. It's an extension of cultivating the awareness, and I might say it's the most direct way towards enlightenment. It combines all of my messages. Specifically, it addresses the major driving force that pushes a human constantly through separation: the desire to feel feelings. Having understood this principle, and having understood that you can bring forth each and every feeling from within yourself, you realize that you do not need any outer circumstances to instill any feeling in you! Having this understanding and practicing it, well, this is the road to liberation.

But there is more to cultivating the light body, and we will go deeply into that today.

We have spoken about Uru and the compression and hypnosis that the group of Uru has conducted on the entities that chose the incarnation experience. The hypnosis was specifically required to eventually make you believe that you are made up of matter. Therefore, you came to the belief that you are a physical body.

As a result of this hypnosis, a part of your consciousness that was already compressed was split off. This split off part connected on the atomic structure of the physical matter of your biological life form – specifically on the DNA. Of course it was known by Uru that there had to be a release mechanism, for otherwise you would've been bound to matter for eternity. That's just the nature of hypnosis. A release mechanism had to be established. But this, say, "key," couldn't be public. If others could have come to know which key would set you free from your hypnosis, well, then they would have interfered – as it has always happened throughout the history of separation.

So, there had to be a secret and unique key for each and every entity. This secret key, guess what that is? Well, I call it *the signature of your true self*. What is the signature of your true self? First, it is based on the feeling of "I exist," just as you have experienced in the first segment of this session. The feeling of "I exist" is on one hand grounded in the bliss of pure consciousness, but it has a singular awareness to it that is absolutely unique. That is why it is a super personal feeling. It just applies to you. If you meet another entity and you try to say or feel "I exist" on behalf of the other, it just doesn't work. You know it's fake, it doesn't work – you cannot become another entity. You exist, and the other entity also exists, but you cannot change roles. It just doesn't work.

Apart from the bliss and singular awareness of yourself, the signature contains even more. It contains the realized wisdom of the true self from all of its experiences. All of this combines into a multi-dimensional, say, "humming sound." This is the signature of your true self.

A crucial fact concerning the feeling of "I exist" is that it is the same for the true self and all of its emanations, or better said, it's "similar enough" so that the true self and its emanations recognize each other as being one. What is the mechanism of how entities know from which true self they come from? They know it through the resonance of the feeling of "I exist."

That is the beauty of the signature of a true self. That is the beauty of the key Uru had chosen to implant in you. But of course, you had the task to come to the choice of wanting to go beyond separation as a human entity, as an incarnated entity. You had to have the braveness to open up totally. You had to have the endurance to face the dragon, and to finally find your true self – without running away or shying away from the intensity of the feelings.

Good. Now, let's see how we can apply this key in principle. But before we do, I ask you to truly make a choice that you want to stay embodied – if that is your choice. Choose to stay embodied, even if you loosen or end the hypnosis – and be it only partially. Make the choice, the deep choice that you want to stay.

*

Good.

Now we'll play a bit of music.

(*Music plays*)

Once again, we go into the Light Body Exercise. I challenged you to do this every morning for the last few weeks. I'm sure everybody has done it, so you are all profound in the experience of it. So, in this session, we can go a bit faster through the initial steps.

First, become aware of your true self. It is so close today, oh it is!

Now, hold the intent to have a light body, and the true self joins in with this intent.

Feel the light of the light body all around your physical body and within your physical body. The signature of your true self is contained in this light, just as bliss is contained in this light.

Become aware of the feeling of safety. Right now, you are totally safe. I would say, you have never been safer. Feel this feeling throughout your physical body, your mind, your emotional body. You are safe.

Now add the feeling of love. Breathe it in. It's in the light all around you, just become aware of it. It's just there for you, waiting to be accepted and felt. Feel the love on every level of your physical being.

Now add the feeling of clarity. You know that you know.

Now join all of this into the feeling of bliss. In this now moment, nothing is lacking, everything is perfect and in fulfillment. I call that bliss.

Now take the dimmer and increase the bliss by a factor of ten, turn the dimmer one notch.

Once again, turn the dimmer one notch. We have bliss times one hundred. When you are exposed to this kind of bliss, everything human you are hanging onto is, in a way, becoming meaningless.

And for the third time, turn the dimmer one more notch.

We have bliss times a thousand.

Breathe it in.

Be it.

In a way, we have prepared you throughout all these weeks for this final session. Some of you have already guessed, and today the puzzle pieces will fall into place. While you are in this wonderful bliss, become aware of the skeleton of your physical body. Let it come in resonance with the signature of your true self. The signature is all around you. It is in your body. It is even in your bones. Allow the skeleton to come into resonance with the signature of your true self.

When the skeleton picks up this vibration, you might say the vibration stays very long with you, even when you go back to your normal daily life. That's because the skeletal bones are so dense that once they pick up the resonance, they "vibrate" for a long time. And the bones vibrate the beautiful remembrance of the signature of your true self throughout all of your body.

Now I want you to become aware of the lowest rib on the left side of your chest; you might even touch it. Become aware of that bone, and place your awareness inside the bone, into the bone marrow.

We are going on a journey now. Feel the signature of your true self in this rib. As said, the signature is contained in the light; it is everywhere and shines throughout your physical body.

In the bone marrow there are stem cells. They are producing the red blood cells. Pick one such stem cell. Imagine it. It's protected by the rib. See that cell and place your awareness directly into it.

The cell is a wonderful world in itself, but we do not investigate here, we just go straight towards the nucleus and into the nucleus. Here you have all the strands of DNA; these long, long strands. Pick one of them. Pick one of them, glide along that strand, and then choose one of its atoms.

The hypnosis that Uru had applied on you was severe, as was the compression. I always use the analogy of an atomic explosion when trying to describe it, and the hypnosis was of the same intensity, for here, down at the atomic level, the energies are enormous. You tear apart a few atoms and you have an atomic explosion. Now, if you want consciousness to believe it is of matter, well, then the hypnosis must create a similar strong bond.

As you glance at the atom that you have picked, you might sense a layer around it which is the hypnotized consciousness of you. Of course, I'm speaking in images, but it helps you to understand what went on.

This hypnotized consciousness is like in a deep, deep, deep dream, continually saying to itself, "I am as my surroundings are. I am as this atom, I am of matter." This is what binds you to physicality. Here is the point where the rubberband is attached that pulls you back whenever you go out, beyond the normal human consciousness. It pulls you back, sooner or later, for this is still your consciousness. It is anchored here for a reason.

The reason, of course, is that you should choose on the deepest level of your beingness to finally let go of the belief in separation.

But as you also choose embodied ascension, it is not just about releasing this hypnotized consciousness by the magic of the key you have! It is about releasing it slowly, slowly, slowly, so that you can maintain a physical appearance in the worlds of separation!

Now, let the light of your true self and its signature touch the part of your consciousness that is hypnotized into the belief "I am of matter." As you do, it can slowly, slowly wake up, like a child that had a long dream. It doesn't know where it is, but here is the beauty: it recognizes its signature – the "I exist"! And as it does, it feels safe, it feels love, it feels the clarity, and it *knows* what to do. In a way, it bonds again with your overall consciousness. Actually, it becomes the link between the light body and the matter of the physical body. But now it's a bond that is not chaining your consciousness to a physical vessel. Quite the contrary! This new bond allows your physical vessel to react to all of your intents. That is the magic of the light body. In this way, your light body becomes partly light, partly matter.

All this happens naturally. Please, do *not* interfere here in any way other than being aware of the signature of your true self!

From this one atom that is waking up, the resonance spreads. We are here, in a stem cell of your bone marrow and you might imagine what it means if this stem cell then creates new blood cells which are circling all around your physical body, always humming the signature of your true self, waking up slowly, slowly all of the rest of the body. Isn't that beautiful?

Now come back to the awareness of all of your physical body. All of what I have just described is going on behind the scenes as you surrender to this most simple Light Body Exercise. It's a non-doing; it's fulfillment; it's just becoming aware of what already is.

Once again, feel the bliss in your physical body; feel the signature touching you, caressing you everywhere.

*

In "The Lucid Dreamer," I have spoken about the "Song of the Dragon." Or better said, I started to prepare the ground to be able to speak about it. And of course, in the last nine weeks we further prepared the ground, so you can now grasp its meaning. What is the Song of the Dragon? Well, actually it is beyond words. It needs to be experienced, but I'll try my best to convey a little bit of it to you.

The first aspect is that the term *Song of the Dragon* itself is a trigger. So, I ask you right now to feel into the term *Song of the Dragon*. Feel into it.

An image might come up. An image of a mighty creature, intoning a song, a sound, of love and beauty.

Maybe the Song of the Dragon is a message from the future-you that is already ascended, that is reaching back in the apparent time to tell you, "Fear not, all is well."

Another aspect of the Song of the Dragon is the fact that, just like the dragon itself, it is also a bridge in consciousness.

We have investigated what happens when the true self hums or sings its signature to the human. This is still happening, and you can feel the signature of your true self throughout your body. But this is not a one way street. You as a human have so much wisdom to share! Actually, it is a wisdom that *exceeds* the wisdom of the true self. Why?

You have come to the understanding of the final letting go.

You have come to the understanding of what it means that all is within.

You have realized what it means to exist beyond identification, be it an identification as a human or even as a true self.

That is a true wisdom.

It is monumental!

And this wisdom has a resonance to it that you could sing or hum. The sound of you combined with the sound of your corporeality, of your story as a human and your wisdom – you could sing that back to the true self.

And when you do that, when the signature of your true self joins with your sound of the human, then the true Song of the Dragon arises and resounds through all of creation.

So, why not do it right now?

Feel again into the sound of your human wisdom, of your human beingness, just as you have done in the first segment of this session. Feel it – the essence of your human story, the essence of your physical body. Feel the essence of all the wisdom realized by you. It's a song that you sing to your true self. And it's a sound that you radiate towards your true self. As you do, you might say that both ends of the bridge are humming, are singing together. They are joining their song. The signature of the true self and the wisdom of the human, they meet, they unite, and they dance together. They become whole and complete.

This is the Song of the Dragon. It is a highly personal song. Feel that.

Your Song of the Dragon is personal, because it carries the scent of the specific journey you have taken and the true self has taken. But at the same time, it's universal, for the highest wisdom is not affected by anyone's journey.

Feel this dance, the resonances. They are recognizing each other. It can be felt throughout your physical body, and that's a wonderful sensation; a wonderful sensation. It can be felt in all the physical and non-physical components of your human incarnation.

If you surrender to the Song of the Dragon, well, this feeling becomes like a gentle – a very gentle – whole body orgasm. And it's beautiful. It's so different from a normal physical orgasm. A physical orgasm lasts for a few moments, a few seconds, maybe a few minutes. But then you are exhausted and want to sleep afterwards. Sometimes, there's even a kind of hangover. You cannot stand this kind of orgasm for too long.

But this – the Song of the Dragon, the corresponding sensation in your body – is total fulfillment! It is non-exhausting, so you could stay in it as long as you like. And if that is your inner state of being, why would you leave it? To chase a stimulus for a feeling?

It's always a bit risky to talk about things like this, for then this whole body orgasm thing might become a goal; an object that you want to achieve or possess. Please, don't do that. Instead, surrender to your Song of the Dragon, allowing these things to happen naturally.

The Song of the Dragon is pure magic. It defies words, so don't stick to my descriptions. Go into it. Find out for yourself what it means for you.

This is so beautiful.

This is the peace within, the peace with yourself, the peace with All-That-Is as All-That-Is.

This is your song of total liberation, of coming home, of going beyond the beyond.

This is your song of utmost clarity. A clarity that transmutes all residues of doubt. It outshines every doubt, every thought, and every concept.

This is your sound as a sovereign being, and you let it be known to all of existence that it has occurred!

*

Right now, there are many, many paradoxes active. Isn't that weird? Let me point out a few of them.

You still have a physical body, yet you know there is no matter, nor space.

You know that on some levels you are still bound to separation and the hypnosis, but yet at this very moment, you are a free and sovereign being.

You don't do anything actively, yet with every breath that you take, you shape the blueprints to ease the path into embodied ascension and enlightenment.

You know that separation does not exist, yet there are other sovereign beings with whom you can join in suchness.

So many paradoxes – one might even say that right now you are living the paradox.

Thankfully, you are not alone in this, so why not become aware of other entities. You have two dozen sitting here with you in your circle. For the last ten weeks, they have been your peers. You haven't talked much with each other, yet you came to know each other on levels that exceed all words.

So, roam around. Greet the others. Thank the others for the journey that we have experienced together. You might also come across Yeshua or Shakyamuni or whoever is standing around here.

Joining in suchness, being sovereign, being unlimited, without needing or craving any identity or reflection – that is the greatest paradox of all.

So we come to the end of this ten week program, but I don't want you to see this as a linear, finite ten week event. Instead, see it as a spiral. As you come to the end of this program, you might start again from the beginning, but then with so much more experience and so much more wisdom.

So, in the next round you take through this material, if you so choose, you can go much deeper. Every time you come back to this material, you will find new layers of information and of experiences that have escaped you before. You will come back with an ever increased simplicity. Things are getting easier and easier and easier. You realize when I have been talking in metaphors. You stop thinking in linearity and cause and effect. You start thinking in images and feelings and compounds.

So, even though this ten week program now comes to a close, it's just a start. We have come full circle.

For me, Althar, these ten weeks have been of outstanding beauty. We have come so far. I have witnessed so many openings in you! So it was a great honor for me once again to be with you, to share my Song of the Dragon with yours; to join in suchness with you.

Now, it's time for the celebration. I hope you all did your homework and brought some champagne or wine or whatever you prefer. I brought some sparkling fluid light and of course my ultra cool crystal sunglasses. So, enjoy the party! Come back to your physical bodies. Take a deep breath with all of us, and a big thank you to all of us. I'm sure we will meet again.

I am Althar, the Crystal Dragon. Cheers to all of you! Thank you.

*

Made in the USA
Monee, IL
14 July 2023

39258262R00184